V.C.'s OF THE ROYAL NAVY
John Frayn Turner

The Battle of Narvik, 'Operation Wilfred,' H.M.S.
Ark Royal—young people who have heard of these
and other episodes of World War II may not know
much about them, or about the men who were
involved. Many of those who survived—perhaps the
parents or grandparents of some of today's young
people—owed their lives to the action of a man who
risked, maybe lost, his own life to save others. This
book relates the courageous deeds of twenty-four men
who were awarded the Victoria Cross.

H.M.S. "ONSLOW" UNDER FIRE

[See Chapter 14]

Illustrated London News

Fr

JOHN FRAYN TURNER

V.C.'s of the
Royal Navy

WHITE LION PUBLISHERS
London and New York

PREFACE

Few people know the names of the men who won the twenty-four naval V.C.'s in the Second World War. Yet not only their names but also their deeds deserve to be remembered.

Eleven of these men lived and thirteen died winning the Cross of courage. To all of them this book is dedicated. I like to think that it will appeal particularly to younger readers, whose memory of the war may be vague but who will appreciate the spirit of service shown in these true stories of action and adventure.

J.F.T.

ACKNOWLEDGMENTS

I am extremely indebted to the following for permission to adapt material written by them:

Captain R. E. D. Ryder, V.C., R.N., who wrote his own account of *The Attack on St Nazaire*, published by John Murray.

Captain G. B. Stanning, D.S.O., R.N., for his narrative of Narvik in the first chapter.

E. G. A. Thompson, Esq., of the Department of Naval Information, Admiralty, for his help and courtesy.

C. E. T. Warren and James Benson, authors of *Above Us the Waves*, published by George G. Harrap and Co., Ltd.

CONTENTS

1. Bernard Armitage Warburton Warburton-Lee   *page* 9
2. Gerard Broadmead Roope   42
3. Richard Been Stannard   46
4. Jack Foreman Mantle   52
5. Edward Stephen Fogarty Fegen   54
6. Alfred Edward Sephton   62
7. Malcolm David Wanklyn   63
8. Eugene Esmonde   83
9. Thomas Wilkinson   92
10. Peter Scawen Watkinson Roberts
    Thomas William Gould   98
11. Anthony Cecil Capel Miers   108
12. Robert Edward Dudley Ryder
    Stephen Halden Beattie
    William Alfred Savage   117
13. Frederick Thornton Peters   148
14. Robert St Vincent Sherbrooke   151
15. John Wallace Linton   157
16. Donald Cameron   165
    Basil Charles Godfrey Place
17. Thomas Peck Hunter   180
18. Ian Edward Fraser
    James Joseph Magennis   183
19. Robert Hampton Gray   190

ILLUSTRATIONS

H.M.S. "Onslow" under Fire   *Frontispiece*

H.M.S. "Glowworm" rams the German "Admiral Hipper"   *page* 14

Roberts and Gould remove a Live Bomb from H.M. Submarine "Thrasher"   15

Captain B. A. W. Warburton-Lee, V.C., R.N.   48

Lieutenant-Commander G. B. Roope, V.C., R.N.   48

Lieutenant R. B. Stannard, V.C., D.S.O., R.D., R.N.R.   48

Leading-Seaman J. F. Mantle, V.C.   48

Captain E. S. Fogarty Fegen, V.C., R.N.   48

Petty Officer A. E. Sephton, V.C.   48

Lieutenant-Commander M. D. Wanklyn, V.C., D.S.O. and 2 Bars, R.N.   49

Lieutenant-Commander E. Esmonde, V.C., D.S.O., R.N.   49

Temporary Lieutenant T. Wilkinson, V.C., R.N.R.   49

Lieutenant P. S. W. Roberts, V.C., D.S.C., R.N.   49

Petty Officer T. W. Gould, V.C.   49

Commander A. C. Miers, V.C., D.S.O. and Bar, R.N.   49

Commander R. E. D. Ryder, V.C., R.N.   64

Lieutenant-Commander S. H. Beattie, V.C., R.N.   64

Able Seaman W. A. Savage, V.C.   64

Captain F. T. Peters, V.C., D.S.O., D.S.C., R.N.   64

Captain R. St. Vincent Sherbrooke, V.C., D.S.O., R.N.   64

Commander J. W. Linton, V.C., D.S.O., D.S.C., R.N.   64

Lieutenant D. Cameron, V.C., R.N.R.   65

Lieutenant B. C. G. Place, V.C., D.S.C., R.N.   65

Corporal T. P. Hunter, V.C., R.M.   65

Lieutenant I. E. Fraser, V.C., D.S.C., R.N.R.   65

Leading Seaman J. J. Magennis, V.C.   65

Lieutenant R. H. Gray, V.C., D.S.C., R.C.N.V.R.   65

1

A MAN is part of a ship; the ship part of a fleet. Sometimes
a Victoria Cross is awarded to the man for a purely personal action, other times because he is in command of a
ship which has distinguished itself as a fighting unit. The
first V.C. awarded in the Second World War, to Bernard
Armitage Warburton Warburton-Lee, honoured the gallantry both of the man and of his ship.

Captain Warburton-Lee—or "Wash," as he was called
—assumed command of H.M.S. *Hardy* and the whole
Second Destroyer Flotilla in August 1939. The stage was
set. The flotilla sailed to Malta, and spent the first six
months of the war operating from Freetown, returning to
the United Kingdom in February 1940, to join the Home
Fleet; Wash with his own ship, the *Hardy*, and the *Hotspur*,
Hostile, *Havoc*, and *Hunter*.

Tuesday, April 2, 1940, marks the start of the operation. The officers of *Hardy*, and other Home Fleet ships,
had realized that sooner or later some of them would be
bound to encounter the Arctic waters and fiords of northern Norway. So no one was surprised in the *Hardy*'s wardroom when "Operation Wilfred" was announced. It was
to be a minelaying venture in Vest Fiord, inside the Lofoten
Islands. Part, not all, of the Second Destroyer Flotilla received orders to escort five minelaying destroyers and then

to stay in the neighbourhood and warn Norwegian or other friendly shipping of the field.   Warburton-Lee was senior officer in charge of the whole affair, to be conducted simultaneously with at least one other minelaying effort southward. It all seemed simple.

Hardy left the comparative sanctuary of Scapa Flow at 1800 on April 2, bound for Sullom Voe in the north of the Shetlands. East of the Orkneys, Wash looked back from the bridge of the *Hardy* to see an enemy air raid on the Fleet anchorage at Scapa, which they had left only an hour or two earlier. A handful of German planes ventured over those heavily protected waters, encircled by barren islands. A barrage of fire was flung into the sky and suspended there, it seemed; the northern night became ablaze.

First glimpse of Sullom Voe came early next morning: an uninviting sight, too. The *Calcutta*, the R.A.F. parent ship *Manela*, and an oiler composed a doleful trio of ships in harbour. This was a period of preparation, organizing for an operation which was destined to be overshadowed by a successor. Apart from ceaseless gales and a dozen-or-so air raid warnings daily, the Shetlands provided peace for two or three days, while Operation Wilfred was delayed.

Meanwhile, *Esk* arrived with *Ivanhoe*, *Icarus*, and *Express*. With *Hardy*, *Hotspur*, *Havock*, and *Hunter*, the little fleet numbered eight. Later on Friday night they received orders to rendezvous with *Renown* at 0700 next morning north of the Shetlands. This came as a surprise to at least some of the *Hardy*'s officers, who had no intimation or idea that the heavyweight *Renown* would be at sea. Perhaps there would be a real 'prize fight' after all.

Hardy set sail at 0300 on Saturday morning, April 6. Although Friday had been so fine, now a southerly gale blew, and navigating the ship through the unlighted booms of Sullom Voe proved difficult in the dark wild night. She made the rendezvous with *Renown* as arranged at 0700, but by this time a considerable sea surrounded her and she was rolling heavily. No morning for a full breakfast, though some of them managed one. Several G-class destroyers screened the *Renown*. The battleship signalled to *Hardy* that *Glowworm* would also take part in the operation but had gone off to try and trace a man who had been washed overboard. Men mattered—although this was war. She would rejoin later.

The C.-in-C. who was flying his flag in *Renown*, told *Hardy* she was to rendezvous with *Birmingham* and *Hostile* off the Norwegian coast. But the sea was worsening if anything, and B.C.I. was evidently worried when the two ships failed to appear. They were due to join the group at 1700 on Sunday and the ships to be detached from the rest at 2000. Saturday and Sunday remain in the memory as a giant gale whipping up continuously from S.S.W. *Glowworm* struggled to rejoin the group, but had to heave-to in the heavy sea.

2000 came, but neither *Birmingham* nor *Hostile*. *Hardy* and the rest detached according to orders, leaving *Renown* S.W. of Vaeroy. Soon afterwards, though, *Birmingham* ploughed on to the scene, and there was a ghostly meeting in a stormswept night. *Hostile* still seemed adrift. One of the other H-class destroyers lost a man overboard. Nothing could be done. It was war with the elements.

Then the weather improved as the *Hardy* turned north inside the Lofoten Islands. These sheltered the ship, which also had the sea on her quarter.

So to Vest Fiord and minelaying. The *Hardy* steamed up the Fiord calmly, sighting a Norwegian patrol vessel which failed to see her in return. In company with the rest of the little assembly, *Hardy* reached the area, and the minelayers started at dawn dropping their mines from inshore outwards. *Hardy* and her three sister ships took up positions at each corner of the area, a rough rectangle thirteen miles by five. *Hardy* had the N.W. corner. Laying started at dawn and finished about sunrise, or before, three-quarters of an hour later. *Hardy* reported the field laid to Admiralty, and the minelayers left the quartet to it.

For a while they steamed up and down at ten knots solely to see the scenery! Snow-covered mountains rose to the east as far as the horizon; the sun climbed higher in a spring sky, tinting distant glaciers an opalescent blue. Warburton-Lee piled on all the clothes he possessed, but still he felt a shiver. It was a bitter contrast to the sweltering South Atlantic he had left only three months earlier; the high-summer heat of January in Freetown.

Although much had been accomplished already that day, it was still early morning on the 8th of April. About an hour after *Hardy* started her 'scenery patrol' a small motor fishing boat appeared from northward, and a moment or two later *Hunter* reported that she was speaking to a Norwegian patrol vessel which had agreed to help her. The *Hardy* stopped the fishing boat and hailed her in English and German, but with no result. The same thing happened twice more before breakfast and three times afterwards. In no case could Wash be sure that the crews had understood the situation, as Norwegian naturally seemed to be the only language any of them could comprehend. At 0930 a more sizeable boat came alongside. "Guns"— the gunnery officer of *Hardy* and Geoffrey Stanning, a supply lieutenant, jumped down into her and tried to explain what they were doing in Norwegian waters, with the aid of a dilapidated chart the Norwegians produced; none of the British maps were large enough scale for them to read.

The meeting ended amicably, and the boat was duly warned of the position of the minefield. Just as Guns and Stanning returned aboard *Hardy*, a signal came through telling her to leave the minefield and join B.C.I. at maximum speed at a rendezvous point outside the islands. *Hardy* did not know then of the loss of *Glowworm* or of the German expedition to Norway. They heard the latter in the early morning news bulletin the next day.

The brief idyll among the snows and the calm waters of the fiord finished abruptly. *Hardy* and her companions sailed round to the outside of the Lofotens, where the heavy seas seemed never to have stopped. The wind was now nor'-west. It took till 1700 to reach the rendezvous with *Renown*. The minelayers were already back under her wing, with some of the G destroyers too.

With visibility very bad, it took some time to form the screen. The H-class destroyers spent the night patrolling east and west and rolling really uncomfortably. Much more so than the time a little before when the wardroom table tops had come away from their legs, which were firmly tethered to the decks. This was off the Orkneys, but was nothing to the present roll. No one actually became sick, but the whole evening of the 8th was remembered for its acute discomfort. Nor did any one sleep during the night of the 8th–9th. Warburton-Lee remained on duty. Stanning spent the whole night deciphering signals, trying to make some sense of a string of long messages which were coming in very mutilated. Although a supply two-ringer, signals were his subject. He worked in his cabin instead of his office. The latter was on an upper deck, hopeless in such conditions. At least his cabin was dry—even if a succession of personal possessions he had not seen since joining the ship regularly reminded him of their continued existence by falling all around him from the racks over his bunk.

Stanning had his Petty Officer Writer with him all through the night, as the ship lurched at impossible angles. They were just finishing one particular message in case it contained something vital. Stanning intended to go up on the bridge afterwards to report to Wash.

Then at 0400, the ship suddenly went to dawn action stations, amid all the storm. A moment later the ship nearest *Hardy*—presumably *Renown*—opened fire. *Hardy* followed suit. Stanning thought they must be doing firing practice. "What a time to pick," he muttered. Then he realized he would have had warning of it—and that they must be in contact with enemy forces.

"Still a terrible time," he mused, "just before dawn in a raging gale. Come on, P.O., we'd better get up to the bridge and see what's happening."

Stanning, clutching the naval cypher, and the P.O. Writer went forward towards the bridge and saw that the firing came from starboard. As they plodded on through the storm, they ran into Mr McCracken the gunnery officer.

"What's it all about, McCracken?" Stanning shouted, above the gale and gunfire.

"Thought it was an exercise at first," the warrant officer replied, "but we must be up against the Germans."

Stanning nodded, and McCracken clambered down a companionway awash with icy water. In fact there was a lot of ice on the deck, and Stanning, groping along it unsteadily, slipped and dropped the naval cypher A table. It careered down the deck, with the two-ringer chasing it. He overtook the precious book just before it vanished overboard, and retraced his slippery steps to the bridge. As he got there, the enemy had just fired their first salvo; every one aboard waited, wondering where it would drop. Fortunately, no hit was recorded. Stanning just made out the silhouettes of a couple of ships as they lay in vivid relief for the moment after firing. Then all was darkness. Spotting was out of the question. Every other sea came right

H.M.S. "GLOWWORM" RAMS THE GERMAN "ADMIRAL HIPPER"

[*See Chapter 2*]

Illustrated London News

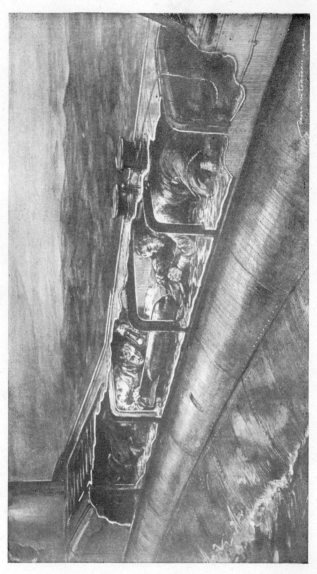

ROBERTS AND GOULD REMOVE A LIVE BOMB FROM
H.M. SUBMARINE "THRASHER"

[See Chapter 10]

Illustrated London News

over the bridge. Conditions were "uncomfortable," as Warburton-Lee understated them to Stanning.

The exchange of salvos continued, with *Hardy* and *Hunter* more or less keeping abreast of *Renown*. But the remainder began to fall back. *Hardy* mustered 18 knots and occasionally 20 or 22. The speeds in the twenties could never be held for more than a minute or two in such seas. *Renown* gradually drew away. *Hardy* just could not stand the pace.

Stanning descended to the chart-house for something— and thought they had been hit. An almighty crash on arrival suggested it, but in fact the ship was just striking an exceptionally heavy sea and Stanning heard it from lower down than previously. Ratings on the lower decks found the noise continuous, deafening.

The action did not last long. Soon the enemy turned away. Opinion in the *Hardy* was inclined to consider that the British force comprised a battle-cruiser (*Renown*), two destroyers (*Hardy* and *Hunter*), and other destroyers; and that they were opposed to an 8-inch and a 6-inch cruiser. Not till long afterwards did they learn that they were mistaken, and the outlines they had seen on the night horizon as the guns flashed were of a battle-cruiser and an 8-inch cruiser.

Before they vanished, however, some salvos fell close to *Hardy* and actually seemed to be straddling *Renown*. The last salvo of all came closer still, so near that those on *Hardy* thought it had burst on their forefoot. In fact, it must just have fallen short. Perhaps it was as well the speed could not be increased beyond about 20 knots, or *Hardy* might have obliged by being those few yards nearer!

Meanwhile, squalls of snow became more frequent, making a mist across the waters, and as *Renown* drew ahead she was blotted prematurely out of sight—from the enemy and *Hardy*. The last impression from *Hardy* was of *Renown* getting close to the enemy, and one definite hit evidenced by a column of black smoke from one or other of the two ships.

Back on the bridge again, Stanning could see perhaps better than the others, although he wore glasses. He carried a spare pair of spectacles in his pocket, and as he wore one pair he cleaned the other. Wash and the rest found it quite impossible to keep binoculars from becoming salty, and so unusable. He made a mental note to have a bowl of warm fresh water on hand for future occasions to counter this difficulty. But in the heat of the battle and chill of the day, no chance came of providing this equipment. The action started—and finished—far too quickly.

The enemy retreated; the elements remained. The squalls became so bad that *Renown* had plunged into the next one by the time *Hardy* emerged from the predecessor. She tried to head *Renown* off, but the battle-cruiser could not be caught. *Hardy* gave up hope of contacting the enemy any more. And as *Renown* turned further and further to starboard it looked like a chase right round the top of Norway. *Hardy* passed some German wreckage soon after losing sight of *Renown*: a life-float, part of a paravane, and an irregular wave-torn patch of oil. So the battle was over; the first battle, anyway. . . .

The Captain glanced at his watch. 0653. Every one on the bridge was wet and excruciatingly cold. Stanning especially, for he had dashed up at 0400 without piling on his whole wardrobe, a fatal omission in weather like this. The enemy had gone out of sight and sound nearly an hour before. So after three hours on the bridge, enthusiasm was dampened more than slightly.

At 0658 *Renown* ordered *Hardy* to break off and return to patrol the southern entrance to the Lofoten Islands. She added that her main W.T. aerials were down, so *Hardy* acted as W.T. link for her during the rest of the day.

Thankfully, *Hardy* turned down wind and sea. Stanning

went back to the bridge to find Warburton-Lee still there. They ate hard-boiled eggs and sandwiches and warmed themselves with coffee. Vaeroy gradually came up on the port bow as breakfast ended.

The ships reached their patrolling positions about 1000, when *Hardy* received a message from the C.-in-C. for Admiralty saying that *Renown* had been in action with a battle-cruiser and an 8-inch cruiser and was still chasing them. She claimed one or two hits. *Renown* reported also that a shell had gone through her bows, without doing any damage or inflicting casualties. The message concluded with what *Hardy* already knew, that *Renown*'s W.T. aerials had been shot away in the combat. The estimate by the *Renown* of the force she had been up against caused astonishment in the *Hardy*'s wardroom, but it was assumed that *Hardy* had underestimated the size of the splashes which fell so uncomfortably close to the ship earlier in the morning.

Much had happened since 0400 and dawn action stations. Wash sipped a cup of cocoa as the patrolling position was reached. The waters were smoother now.

Then at 1130 came the dramatic order from Admiralty *to take three ships and attack Narvik the same evening*. No precise information was included of the forces to be expected there, except that one or two ore ships had landed soldiers. "Exciting but easy" was the initial impression in *Hardy*. Taking *Hotspur*, *Havock*, and *Hunter*, she set sail up Vest Fiord. All that had passed had been but a prelude to the action which was soon to start.

Warburton-Lee began to issue orders for the attack. The time it would be due to start was fixed for 2000, as they could not reach the target much before. Orders included instructions for preparing landing parties, and for an attack from each side of the peninsular on which Narvik lies. It seemed impossible to approach and take the place by surprise, as perfect positions for shore batteries existed on high points down the fiord—and every chance existed of one or two submarines lying up fiord who would also be well placed to fire their torpedoes at an approaching warship before being engaged.

Wash sent for Stanning. The lieutenant was having lunch, but left it willingly.

"Come and sit down, Stanning. What about your meal?" It was characteristic of him to be concerned of things like this, however much he had on his mind.

"Practically finished, sir. Don't worry."

"Right, then. Now look here, I'm thinking of calling at the pilot station at Tranoy to see if it's occupied by the Huns—or if not, to ask whether they've any information that might be useful to us."

Stanning badly wanted to ask if he could go. He had just made up his mind to do so, in fact, when Warburton-Lee went on to ask,

"Which boat would you like to take?"

Stanning smiled; Wash, too.

"Now, I think I should use the skimmer if I were you," Wash advised, "it might be useful in a tight spot. If the place is occupied by the enemy, by any chance, you'd have a better chance of getting away fast in it."

The skimmer, however, had decided otherwise. In the morning's activities, or the storms of the preceding days, its steering wheel had broken off. Moreover, in spite of the united efforts of practically everyone aboard, it refused to start. Stanning was sorry not to have its speed, in case safety had to be sought rapidly. But in another way he did not regret the skimmer defaulting, as he would undoubtedly have got very wet again, and although it was certainly fast it seemed small and shelterless if any one did start firing at him from shore.

The motor boat, too, was out of commission, as it had

met with an accident just before the *Hardy* left Scapa, making it minus a propeller. So it was the starboard sea boat.

Hardy arrived off Tranoy about 1600. Clutching a chart, Stanning boarded the boat. Just as he was going to shove off, the torpedo officer, Heppel, came over to the side and suggested that he should come along, too; Stanning gladly accepted his moral—and physical—support.

They grounded on the nearest point of land and sent the boat round the pier which they could see in the little harbour. Stanning and Torps picked a wary way over seaweed-covered rocks. Soon they saw some of the locals, mostly men, strolling casually down to the pier.

"No Germans about, anyway," Stanning observed with relief.

After the pair got quite near to the inhabitants they realized they were on an island separated from the shore by about fifty yards of sea, with the Norwegians on the mainland. They called up the boat again and were taken over to the pier in her.

Stanning and Torps went ashore purposefully and walked up to the crowd of a couple of dozen men and boys who had gathered by this time.

The Captain focused his binoculars on the scene as he watched from the bridge of the *Hardy*.

Some of the Norwegians spoke a little English.

"Have you seen any Germans?" Stanning asked, then added by way of clarification "—soldiers or ships."

Several of them responded at once. No, they had not seen any soldiers. But Yes, most of them had watched five German destroyers heading towards Narvik that same morning.

Stanning turned excitedly to Torps, and then to the Norwegians.

"How large were they? What size?"

"Bigger than that one," a burly fisherman spoke up quickly, pointing to the *Hardy*.

"How about one of you coming with us and piloting the ship to Narvik?"

There could be no doubt about their feelings; there was a general murmur in the negative and a shaking of heads. Stanning accepted the situation. He unrolled his chart to try to extract a bit of local information from them but found that in his hurry he had picked up the wrong one from the desk on the bridge. All he had in his hands was a small-scale chart of the lower part of the Vest Fiord. It proved quite useless, so they drew pictures in the snow of Narvik and its harbour.

Another of the locals said he was sure he had seen a submarine steam up to Narvik on the surface. He also asserted that the whole area was mined. A small fair boy tugged at Stanning's trousers.

"Not five ships—six," he told them in Norwegian. Although the naval men did not know the language, the meaning was quite clear. It did not occur to them that there could have been five destroyers *and* six more, making a formidable eleven in all.

Some one asked Stanning if they were going to attack Narvik. He shrugged his shoulders and gave a noncommittal answer. The man told them they ought to go and get many more ships before they tried.

The naval party took a friendly farewell and hurried back to the *Hardy*.

By the time they got aboard again they found that the *Hardy*, *Hotspur*, *Havock*, and *Hunter* had been joined by *Hostile*, a welcome arrival and addition.

"Come in and tell me all about it," the Captain said.

In the chart house, they explained the situation as it was seen ashore. As the facts of the five enemy destroyers —not to mention any more—and one or more submarines seemed to be fairly established, Wash was faced with a difficult dilemma. He had received orders to attack Narvik, so unless strong and urgent grounds existed against it, he must act accordingly. Admiralty obviously had no idea how strong were the enemy forces in the port, yet to ask for further instructions would mean delaying the operation unreasonably. He had a shrewd suspicion that this might have been timed in association with some other operation down the coast. If that were so, delay might prejudice someone else's success or even their safety. But it did seem doubtful that Admiralty would approve of taking such a risk to the five modern H-class destroyers—a risk which was grave in view of the information that had come to light ashore during that day.

Wash walked up and down the chart house, and his cabin, and the bridge. . . . He turned the possibilities over in his mind. Their intelligence might not necessarily prove reliable, however strongly the Norwegians had insisted that the ships they saw were German destroyers. As Admiralty had issued such specific instructions, it was reasonable and right to suppose that they knew best.

He had not made up his mind yet. As he assessed the pros and cons he remembered the possible unreliability of local information, for when he had been in the South Atlantic on *Hardy*, in company with a couple of other destroyers, the trio were variously reported ashore later as two tankers and a submarine; six destroyers; and two cruisers!

A comparative calm came down on the *Hardy*, accentuated by its contrast from the storm and stress of recent hours and days. Now the stress was mental. Wash thought it all out again. If he decided to attack Narvik and failed, perhaps with the loss of several ships which could ill be spared, he would be bound to be told that he was wrong to go in while aware of the heavy opposition. Should he withdraw, however, he could well be asked why he did so on the word of locals or small boys when Admiralty had given him his orders. Five, ten, fifteen minutes, and a right-angle of the clock. The crew of the *Hardy* chatted in groups, mostly below decks, for still the snow flurried slightly across her bows. Half an hour after the uneasy calm, Warburton-Lee emerged. He had decided.

Stanning knew in his heart what the captain would do; when Wash burst in on him, it was confirmed. Purpose was written on his senior's face, tempered by the relief of an awkward decision made. Right or wrong, the time for thought was past, and for action soon to come.

"I'm attacking at dawn, Stanning, with high water. We can't manage it earlier. The time spent off Tranoy means that we could still get to Narvik tonight, but I think it will be far better to go up before dawn. That way there'll be more chance of surprise—and we'll certainly need that element in our favour. One thing more, though. I want you to get a cypher through to Admiralty at once. I'll let you have it in a minute. I intend to pass on all the information you and Torps got at Tranoy."

"Aye, aye, sir. And may I say how glad I am about your decision?"

"Hope you'll still be this time tomorrow." And with that, Wash was gone to prepare for the assault.

In order to give any possible hostile observers ashore the impression that they had gone off to get reinforcements— as had been advised at Tranoy—*Hardy* and the others sailed down-fiord. Operational orders were not changed to any appreciable extent; the four consorts were given the gist of the changed situation, though, and told the time of the attack.

A second lull before the storm of the morrow. The first, awaiting the decision to attack; the second now, counting off the hours till the actual assault. The lull even seemed to spread to Stanning's cyphering activities. So he went down to the wardroom and gossiped with a group of officers. He could not get any sleep, which every one wanted, as messages might come through at any time—and anyway the sense of expectancy put it out of the question. Aquilina, the wardroom cook, carried on as usual, producing a respectable supper.

"Thank God for Aquilina," voiced Torps. "I think he'd have managed to whip up soup, joint, and sweet in the middle of Trafalgar." Stanning was sipping his coffee when a voice over inter-com called,

"Will Lieutenant Stanning please report to the Captain?"

Wash was still worried about the next day. "I wonder what Admiralty think about all this, Stanning? It's a nice point balancing the risk involved against a delay in the attack."

"I know how you feel, sir, but if it's any consolation I'd like to tell you that the whole ship's company would be desperately disappointed if the attack weren't to come off now."

"Thanks. That's good to know."

They chatted for some time. Then Stanning left Wash and went up on the compass platform. It was 2130. Dusk had just passed. The night was clear and calm. "Admiralty will have got our signal by now," Stanning thought. But Whitehall and the old cobbled forecourt seemed a million miles away. As far as Venus. He glanced up at the planet. The *Hardy* steamed up and down the side of the Vest Fiord near the Lofotens. She was on the northward leg at the moment. Stanning saw the snow-covered peaks on each side quite distinctly: a moonlit white, turning the entire scene into memorable unreality.

Torps told Stanning that he had been on the mess deck explaining exactly how things stood. The crew knew roughly, but it was the thoughtful thing to do.

Stanning finally reached his bunk at about 2230—normal bed-time, he thought, but a far-from-normal night. He was dead tired, but could only sleep a little. And he was awake in a trice when called at 0015. The whole ship's company went to action stations before 0030; only a matter of minutes after midnight Stanning moved up to the bridge. The *Hardy* was still sailing up Vest Fiord. The two-ringer found himself busy for a time installing the P.O. Writer in the chart-house with the cyphers, which were in Stanning's suitcase, and with paper and pencil ready to take a narrative he would pass by voice-pipe from the compass platform.

This operation over, Stanning went aft again to tell Mr McCracken that he must dump the safes aft in an oil tank if anything happened. This was only routine. He felt no particular premonition.

By the time he had left McCracken it was snowing hard again, and he took about ten minutes or more getting back forward. He arrived back to the bridge just as they altered course to turn up Narvik Fiord. A few minutes later, with visibility rapidly deteriorating, *Hardy* almost ran aground on some ice projecting from the beach, or the snow-clad beach itself—they could not tell which. Torps saw it first. It looked inevitable that they would beach. Somehow the ship swung just in time.

Visibility grew worse. They reduced speed from 15 knots to 12, and burned a fog light. Alterations in course and speed were passed by wireless. No one could have blamed the pilot if the whole quintet had gone ashore, but he seemed quite confident. Midshipman Pope took soundings to see all was well, and Stanning relieved him for a spell while the middy was wanted elsewhere. Later Stanning took Asdic bearings on the beach.

Suddenly a cypher arrived. It was a message from Admiralty giving Wash full liberty of action and assuring

him of Admiralty support. He was delighted. It had
come through just at the right moment, dispatched from
London at 0100, read by him an hour later. It also mentioned that a couple of Norwegian coast-defence ships
might be in German hands. No one bothered much about
the last part of the message. So the operation went full
steam ahead.

Soon afterwards a second signal came through. It was
received very incomplete and mutilated, however, and at
first Stanning could not decipher any of it. It had been
marked "immediate," though, so every effort was made.
The message might be second thoughts on the Admiralty's
part, telling them to call off the operation. But nothing
could be made of it. Luckily a repeat of the cypher came
through presently.

Stanning decoded it and hurried to tell Wash what it
said: "Count up the number of Germans in Narvik, their
guns and their stores!"

"Some one with a sense of humour back home," Wash
said. In fact, it was sent in earnest. "We'll have enough on
our hands at dawn without doing arithmetic," he added.
How right he was! Wash crumpled the paper and it was
whisked away into the depthless night of snow. Paper made
from pulp made from timber of Norway—now fluttering
back towards its native land.

The flotilla of five moved on, through thicker snow;
nearer to Narvik; nearer.

Just as the pilot was convinced they had reached the
port, land veered into view on the port bow and also
ahead. But it turned out to be only a small inlet to the
south-west, and not Narvik at all. Up till now, they had
seen not a sign of local civilization or—more remarkable
still—no hint at all of the enemy. It seemed reasonable to
suppose that if the Germans were at Narvik in any force

they would have had a destroyer patrolling the lower part of the fiord, or at least a submarine anchored in the channel. It was just possible, of course, that the flotilla had passed such a patrol in the bad visibility. One or two of the *Hardy's* officers even thought Heppel (Torps) and Stanning must have got hold of the wrong end of the stick at Tranoy and that there really were not many Germans at Narvik. Hopes even began to revive of a landing party, hardly in question with half a dozen large enemy destroyers in port.

"I've just remembered," Stanning suddenly exclaimed, "it's my birthday—to-day's the 10th, isn't it?"

"Well, I'll be——" Wash responded on the bridge. "Chances are that you won't forget how you spent this particular one. How about a bottle of champagne to celebrate?" He was just getting around to organizing one from below (at 0430 in an Arctic fiord!) when the look-out reported a fishing-boat to starboard, lying off a small wooden pier.

"Signs of life," the Captain said. "May have to forgo that toast to you, Stanning."

A second later they saw a headland on the port bow. "Must be the north side of the harbour entrance, sir," the pilot decided. It was. They had finally stumbled on the harbour very quickly. A merchant ship lay right in the entrance, and there was much more shipping inside the harbour.

"Tell the others to stop engines," Wash said. "We'll go in alone and investigate."

Hardy glided as a ghost into the harbour before dawn. Still no sign of life confronted her. She neared the merchant ship and they saw two guns on the poop.

"Must be British," some one said in the gloom. *Hardy* left her very close to port. Another ship came into sight high aground on the south shore. At that stage they could not make out any more of the confused mass of vessels further in the harbour. Silence and snow fell on the scene. Just before *Hardy* completely passed the supposedly British merchant ship, Stanning saw the black form of a man walking up and down the deck amidships.

"Shall I hail him and ask where the Germans are?"

"No," said Wash, "we don't want to risk waking any one sooner than necessary. Surprise is still on our side."

The town itself was half a mile or more away, but so profound was the quiet as *Hardy* sailed slowly up-harbour, it seemed certain that even a few words spoken loudly would carry across the water and awaken the enemy.

Not even the engines disturbed the quiet, for *Hardy* was drifting now without a sound. Wash was peering through steady snow into the gloom. *Hardy* floated forward.

Suddenly some one shouted: "There they are!"

Two enemy destroyers lay alongside each other right in the middle of the harbour, bows towards the town.

"Can I open fire, sir?" Torps asked quickly.

"Carry on and fire," the Captain called.

Torps volleyed four tubes at them.

Wash ordered: "20 knots" to helm, to take them round the ship in the entrance and out of the harbour. *Hardy* was still alone, of course. As she gathered way, Guns sighted more destroyers alongside the quay. Stanning saw one of the first torpedoes strike the bow of a large merchant ship astern of the two destroyers aimed at. A split second later an explosion from the direction of the two destroyers told that Torps' shooting had been good. Guns ranged his armament on to the fresh batch of destroyers he had seen, but by now they were hardly visible. Spasmodically, for seconds after the big bang, came many more, indicating that magazines must have been hit. Thousands of rounds of ammunition went up in the air.

"Quite a firework display," Stanning shouted, above

the roar. But even as he spoke the words, he thought of the inevitable loss of life they had caused. Wash, too, was quiet.

As *Hardy* turned out of the harbour, they fired three more torpedoes in the general direction of the others, and emerged with only one left.

Hotspur and *Havock* had been sent up towards Rombaks Fiord to see if there were any enemy in the neighbourhood. The other two Wash summoned and told to go past the harbour entrance and fire torpedoes as they went. *Hardy*, meanwhile, was engaging a shore gun on the point north of the harbour which had opened fire. More signs that the Germans were beginning to stir themselves came from the harbour itself. They were firing small stuff—not more than twelve pounders—towards *Hardy* and her two consorts. Wash could see it coming as it was all tracer. He could not do much about it, but the haphazard aim comforted him and the others.

Hardy was within a mile of Narvik, yet neither side could see the other. The Germans fired blindly out of the harbour; *Hardy* shot equally at random into it. *Hardy* silenced the guns on the point. That was the end of the first attack. No damage to the Navy—so far.

The small stuff continued to etch its way across the sky and cascade into the waters around them.

"Better put on tin hats," said Wash.

The tracer did not seem likely to do any harm, however, and soon afterwards they had all taken their hats off again—including Wash. They were going over to the offensive again.

Hardy and the other two began to re-form ready for another attack. *Hotspur* and *Havock* had returned from Rombaks Fiord by this time, reporting "nothing there"; so now they had all five for the attempt. *Hardy* kept close to the entrance to the harbour in case anything tried to leave. She circled in front of the entrance for the second time, firing her guns at enemy flashes when they lit the snow-backed port behind the ships. Heavier gunfire came from Narvik now—from the probably damaged destroyers. Wash was anxious to find out what damage had been inflicted, as they had heard many louder explosions since the first batch earlier. But they could see nothing of the result.

Not only heavy guns aimed at them now. As *Hardy* crossed the entrance to the southward, torpedoes tore through the fiord towards her. Some came very near, too close for comfort, and one actually seemed to go underneath the ship. Stanning counted six torpedoes, but others saw more and said three went under the vessel. However, none of them hit, nor did they explode. They could be heard from the deck of *Hardy* as they went ashore on the beach opposite, whirring weirdly, mechanically, as they tried to scramble up the sand. Each of the five H-class destroyers took a turn at the entrance to the harbour, then finally they all withdrew.

Wash asked the others for details of damage or casualties, and how many torpedoes they had left.

"No damage, no casualties," came back the signals. And *Hostile* said she still had a full load of torpedoes.

Mansell told Wash that *Hardy* had a small hole in the after-funnel, and confirmed that three torpedoes had gone under them. Every one was in high spirits. The second stage of the battle was over, and still no damage had been sustained. All enemy guns seemed to have ceased fire fairly early in this latter attack; perhaps all opposition had been silenced.

Wash called in his officers. "What do you think about things now?" he wanted to know. "What's it to be—withdraw or go in again?"

They all agreed it would be better to carry on. They did not know how much damage had been done, nor what enemy forces still survived. It would be ridiculous to withdraw in face of no further opposition. Every one felt they ought to try and estimate the weight of the enemy and report it back to Admiralty.

Wash summed up: "Glad to have your views. I don't mind saying that I'm anxious no one should get torpedoed after having eluded them a couple of times. But as so many seem to have been fired at us already it does look as if there can't really be many more on tap. So on that score, I should say let's go ahead again. And if we were still in doubt, *Hostile* still has her load, and I want to let her have a turn."

A chorus of approval greeted his decision, the second difficult one he had been forced to take within twenty-four hours. All the while that they had been considering the latest situation, the *Hardy* was steaming slowly down-fiord. When the Captain made up his mind, they were a way from the harbour entrance. He turned her round, and at first the entrance could not be found again—just as it had eluded them before the initial assault. Then they saw the old fishing-boat near the wooden pier. Soon they were at the entrance. The harbour looked in a chaotic state, but it was difficult to discover the damage from previous attacks. Now at any rate they saw that the supposedly British ship near the entrance had been sunk, with her stern pointing mountain-wards, high out of the water.

Then there came a terrible shock.

Wash suddenly sighted three enemy warships heading straight towards them from the direction of Rombaks Fiord. He took them to be a cruiser and two destroyers—and gave the order: "Engage."

Hardy opened fire on them at the simultaneous second that they attacked. Visibility had increased only a matter of minutes before—or the flotilla might have collided with the three enemy vessels. Whether the first was a cruiser or leader destroyer, it certainly looked larger than the others.

Wash thought quickly after the first exchange of salvos. Then he ordered the signal to withdraw—a red Verey light—at thirty knots.

Clark protested that *Hardy* was hitting them, and wanted to stay. But before another word was possible two more ships appeared ahead.

Cross said: "*Birminghams.*"

They were four miles off and looked like our own cruisers. But Stanning snatched up his glasses and caught sight of hoods on their funnels.

"Not ours," he said tersely. Then he thumbed through the pages of the 'Janes' which were on the bridge. "Large German destroyers," he added with animation.

That clinched it. They were in a tight corner. The two Germans ahead turned sharply to port and opened fire. *Hardy* engaged them both, leaving the other three to her rear ships. It must have been at this moment, when *Hardy* was taking on the two ahead and Wash wanted the others to tackle the three remaining, that he made the last signal of his life:

"Keep on engaging the enemy . . ."

Hardy made a report about the strength of the enemy. She was being hit by now, and damage was done. The firing was uncomfortably accurate. Stanning felt several hits forward, then a tremendous tearing explosion on the bridge. Most of them were there.

Stanning was stunned for the second. He was thrown into the air, then fell on the gyro compass, near the Asdic set. Cross had been at his desk; Clark on the starboard side of the bridge forward; Wash by the Asdic set; Gordon-Smith behind the gyro compass. Torps was about too. Stanning felt as if he had been carrying a tray of china and dropped the lot.

He came to. Wash was lying on his back, breathing, but

with a ghastly gash in the side of his face and another on his body. The pilot lay on his face, down the step from the compass platform. He was kicking. Stanning thought that the bridge had suddenly become very dirty. A strong smell of cordite fumes hung in the air, both compasses were broken, and the chart table could not be seen.

Stanning felt a surge of loneliness; it seemed as if he must be the only one alive in the ship. Yet the vessel still steamed at speed, making for the southern shore.

"If I don't do something quickly we'll be on the bricks."

He hailed the wheelhouse, received no answer, and came to the conclusion he would have to go down there himself. He must have had his weight on the right foot, for as he put his left foot to the deck he found he could not walk on it. He recalled the terrific jerk of the explosion. He hopped across the bridge. On the way he rolled Pilot over on his back in the narrow alley by the torpedo control, and left him as comfortable as he could.

He slid down to the wheelhouse, which was in a shambles, and saw debris of clothes and belongings but no bodies, certainly not the coxswain's. Stanning wrenched the wheel to starboard to try to stop the ship being beached. He was surprised to find it to be working. The ship had been darkened so there was nowhere to look out to see what effect the wheel was having; but luckily the iron cover of the centre square window was hanging free, and by pushing it open he could peer through. *Hardy* had answered the helm so efficiently that she was swinging fast to starboard and the enemy. Stanning put some port wheel on and had another look. For a couple of minutes or so he went on steering the ship down the fiord, having to hop to the square window, lift up the flap, and look out at intervals to get an idea of direction.

While he was still steering, A.B. Smale appeared in the doorway.

"All right, are you, Smale? Come and take the wheel, so I can get back to the compass platform."

Stanning was glad to see the seaman, especially as he knew him to be utterly reliable. As soon as he reached the platform he realized that something would have to be done within the next minute or so—for the ship was nearly abreast of the German destroyers. Stanning saw that both numbers one and two guns were out of action, although some of the after-guns seemed still to be firing.

The question was whether to try and rush past the Germans or ram them.

"Probably the proper thing," Stanning thought to himself. Then he remembered about the other ships and hurried over to the starboard side of the bridge to try and see what was happening to them. He never saw them, for just as he got to that side a whole salvo seemed to strike the engine room and the boilers. A cloud of steam spurted and spluttered. The *Hardy* began to slow down. Stanning assumed the entire engine room must have been obliterated—but actually only one man was wounded by that particular salvo. Steam must have been emitted in so many places at once that no one had been hurt by it escaping under pressure.

But Stanning did not know all that, nor could he believe that there were more than a score of survivors aboard all the ship. No one could be sent to see what had happened. Another decision had to be made. What should he do with the ship? He decided to put her ashore. It seemed the obvious and only thing to do.

In a matter of seconds all the various pros and cons flitted through his brain. He tried to weigh them fairly. Calm thought was not easy. 'The ship is certainly no more use as a fighting unit, and few people can still be alive. All right; one point in favour of beaching her. But it is wrong to put a ship ashore in enemy territory, where the Germans

might be able to get at some of the secret gear and the
cyphers. One-all. What should I do? I don't know how to
sink the ship myself. Even if I did, I couldn't possibly cope,
with this wretched foot.' To remind him, it suddenly gave
a twist of pain. 'I ought to be able to destroy most of the
secret stuff with Smale's help. The Germans will take some
time to get to the ship ashore—longer than if she were
drifting about the fiord which is all she's fit for now. Poor
old *Hardy*.'

Not a second could be lost. The ship was losing speed
quickly now, and Stanning wanted to reach a group of
houses a few hundred yards inland. There was the prospect
of shelter. As he put the port wheel over to turn the *Hardy*
gently in towards the shore, one of the houses was hit by a
shell and set on fire. The ship glided to the shallows.

Just then Heppel burst in. Stanning had wondered what
had been happening to him since last seeing him. In fact,
he had been hit in the face by a small splinter before the
disaster on the bridge and had gone to give first-aid to
himself. As soon as the bridge was hit, a signalman told
Heppel that every one there was dead—though they were
not—and that the wheelhouse was out of action. Heppel
had hurried to the engine room to tell them to change over
to the after steering position. But when they started to
steer they found that the ship was still being steered from
forward. Heppel returned to the bridge, found Smale
there, and asked him what was happening. Smale said he
was getting helm orders from up top, from Stanning.

So Heppel found Stanning on the compass platform and
stood for a second regaining his breath.

"What are you doing, man?" he asked.

"Going on the bricks."

"You can't do that. Midships. Starboard 20."

But Stanning put his elbow in the voice pipe, so Smale
never got the order.

"We must. She won't go any more."

"What do you mean?" Heppel was unaware of the position, obviously.

"No more steam," Stanning said simply.

Before the discussion could be continued *Hardy* reached shallow water and grounded unbelievably gently. People at the back of the bridge began to come to life again. Several signalmen scrambled up as Stanning returned to the bridge.

He knew he must destroy the cyphers and the A.S. cabinet and bridge set. He still did not know that almost all the officers were alive. Heppel had defiantly gone off to fire his last torpedo at the enemy. Stanning got up the flag lockers and called some sailors by name to come and help him. Then he sent the Chief Stoker off to find Mr McCracken and help him throw the safes aft into the oil tank outside the Captain's cabin.

"Pope!" Stanning shouted to one of the midshipmen, "go and get the cyphers out of the chart-house, shove them in the weighted bag, and chuck them overboard as far aft as you can." Previously, Pope had rushed to the wheel-house and put the engines at full speed astern when he had seen the ship going aground. He did not know there was no steam.

Mansell came up to Stanning. "The Asdic cabinet's been blown out of the ship." He confirmed later that the set on the bridge had been destroyed.

Up on the bridge the doctor was attending to Pilot.

"The telegraphist in radio control on the bridge was pinned in, but Pope levered the place open and let him out," Mansell told Stanning. "What are we going to do now?" he asked. Then answering himself: "I want to get the motor-boat out."

They both went down on the starboard side, but the after-thread of the davit was twisted and they could not turn the boat out. In any case it was full of holes and had no rudder or propeller. They wheeled round to the skimmer on the other side under No. 3 gun-deck. Normally it had to be manhandled under the torpedo davit, so was not easy to extract. But they had to find something which would float. Stanning and the others sat down and started to unreel the wire for the torpedo davit.

Stanning looked up and saw Pilot coming down from the bridge alone, seriously wounded but just able to walk. He sat down beside Stanning, lit a cigarette. Stanning had to go on unreeling. A moment later Pilot suddenly began choking. Stanning thought he must be dying, for he lay quite still. The lieutenant got some one to put him in the narrow cross passage.

By then they found they could not get the skimmer out. The stanchion supporting the gun deck was so badly bent the boat could not be moved past it. Mansell suggested a Carley float for taking the wounded ashore. The enemy were shelling the ship and shore spasmodically. Several shells hit the beach near those of the crew who were already ashore and filing up the enemy beach in a thin black stream. The shelling of the ship intensified. They decided to abandon her at once. Stanning went aft between the torpedo tubes and took off his oilskins. A shell burst on the "Chief's seat" abaft the after-funnel. This must have been what killed the chief stoker. . . .

Stanning was scared now. He jumped into the sea fully dressed except for his oilskins. His first urgent concern was to swim clear of the ship and avoid the shells. The water was icy. He tried to comfort himself that there was not much of him above water to hit. He had blown up his rubber lifebelt and found he was swimming quite well. Much sooner than he expected he touched ground only about fifty yards inshore from the ship. He could not wade in and had to finish the journey on his stomach.

All the others had got ashore by now. Stanning realized he was being left behind and could not catch up the others. He shouted to two torpedo-men ahead, and they dropped back to help him. He still had a hundred yards of foreshore to negotiate, covered with rocks and pools. 'Just the place for a child to play,' he thought. The pain from his injured foot was agonizing. Even with the two men's help he felt he would never make it, and told them to push ahead again. Somehow they got Stanning to dry land, or snow-clad shore. At the top of the beach a path fifty yards long to the road lay waist deep in snow. They supported Stanning between them and at last they reached the road. They trudged along it, and another path deep in a drift, then finally reached a wooden house.

The three of them groped inside. They saw dozens of men, a stench of bodies, the tang of burnt cordite, the dankness of soaked clothes. The early arrivals had dressed themselves in the clothes and bedclothes of the owners, Mrs Christiansen and her daughter. The two women were now downstairs tearing the curtains from the windows, ripping up the carpets and rugs to wrap the shivering sailors in; they ransacked their larder for food and gave almost every one a slice of bread and butter.

Stanning and his two sailors merged into the rest of the room. The company stayed like this for some minutes, sorting themselves out, talking things over. The first shock of the ship's loss was now over. They were beginning to think what it had meant, who was alive—and who dead.

Stanning's foot got more and more painful. Some one cut his boot off, and the foot swelled up like a football. He hobbled over to Dr Waind.

Then Geoffrey Stanning plucked up courage to ask the question which had been worrying him most:

"What happened to Wash?" He looked straight into

Waind's eyes, waiting to tell from them whether hope still survived.

"He was almost dead before he left the ship, old chap, but they got him on to the Carley float. He died on the way. . . ."

Stanning was silent for a second. Five words, like his signal: "Keep on engaging the enemy."

Waind went on: "Guns and Flags must have been killed outright."

"Thanks for telling me," said Stanning. Then he sent a message to Heppel to go back to the ship, fetch Pilot, and make sure that all the books in the Captain's cabin aft were destroyed.

They were in a peculiar position and obviously could not stay indefinitely crowded in the house which the Christiansens had now abandoned to them. Yet no one was fit to go far, and many had no boots. They really expected the Germans to send a party ashore from one of their destroyers to take them prisoner, or else get a detachment from Narvik to go by road. But nothing seemed to be happening yet. Stanning sat outside the house, as it was fairly warm now. He could speak German so he thought he could best negotiate with any enemy. At the moment he sat down, he saw—and heard—an explosion somewhere down the fiord. A column of black smoke shot high above the mountains. Although he did not know it then, *Hostile* was torpedoing *Rauenfels*. Nor did he or the others discover that *Hunter* was badly damaged and that a few minutes afterwards *Hotspur* herself was hit and her steering gear jammed; she was heading for *Hunter* at the time and rammed the other destroyer fair and square. bowling her over.

Meanwhile, *Hardy* was burning forward, and her small ammunition exploded intermittently, echoing in bursts across the beach and fiord. On the other side of the fiord,

Stanning could just make out through the trees a German destroyer ashore as the *Hardy* was, with no sign of life near her.

Then some one shouted, pointing to the *Hardy*: "Look, a man walking about on the foc'sle. Must be either Pilot or a missing stoker."

Stanning knew the shape of the man. It was Pilot. He was still alive. He hoped Heppel had got back to the ship by now and would bring Pilot ashore.

A lorry and a car drew up outside the house. Stanning was sure they would contain Germans. But a small man in spectacles hurried up the snowy path. He proved to be a doctor.

"You ought to put some more clothes on," he told Stanning, who was drying himself and his gear in the sun, "and I'll get you to hospital. I've got a cottage hospital about fifteen miles away, at Ballangen. I can take all your wounded."

"Thanks. Will you come in and help Styles, a chief stoker? He's in a bad way with a fractured skull."

The man examined Styles.

"Too bad to move," he pronounced.

In fact, Styles was dying.

The worst cases were taken out to the lorry, which whisked away to Ballangen. After ages, it seemed, they heard the lorry returning. Stanning longed to go to hospital as his foot was aching almost unbearably. Heppel was seen on his way ashore with Pilot. A dozen of them got into the lorry—all the wounded that were left—and then Pilot appeared. He was put into the vehicle carefully, and though still a terrible sight once more smoked a cigarette contentedly. The Germans could not kill him. Even Stanning never expected to see him again. Pilot lay on the floor of the van, with his feet against the rear door, as they bumped along the snowy road. An hour passed before Ballangen came into view. Beyond the village they turned into a square three-storey building which was the hospital. A comforting aroma of antiseptics suggested they would be in good hands. They were told that the worst cases must go on to Harstad, a better-equipped hospital. As they all waited on benches in the passage until they could be examined, Stanning saw that several unwounded ratings from the *Hardy* had got to the hospital in the first load. He enquired from someone on what grounds they had managed it, and was told they had complained of frostbite. He knew there was nothing wrong with them at all and felt rather ashamed—especially as he thought of Warburton-Lee.

Stanning looked down at his watch from habit. It registered 7.12—the minute he had jumped from the *Hardy*. Wash must have gone about the same time. The pain from Stanning's foot seared through him. The doctor did not see him till about four, nearly nine hours after the battle. Then he had morphia and sank into his first sleep for four nights.

Four days of confusion followed for Stanning, under morphia. On Saturday morning, Heppel and Torps told him of a plan to get away via Tranoy. Almost as they spoke, a colossal crash heralded the opening of an attack on a German destroyer in Ballangen Bay. *Warspite* it was, in the fight. That evening Heppel rushed back into Stanning's room with the news that he had been on board *Ivanhoe*, and that he was taking the unwounded aboard that same night. The wounded would follow the next day. So about 1000 on Sunday, April 14, Stanning and some others were transferred into the lorry, driven down to the little pier, and put into *Ivanhoe*'s boat. Thence to *Ivanhoe*, to *Warspite*, *Woolwich*, and the hospital carrier *The Isle of Jersey*.

It was not until Stanning finally returned to Aberdeen that he heard the full facts of the battle of Narvik.

Hardy and the other destroyers of the flotilla caused havoc to numerous supply ships and transports lying in harbour and repeatedly hit two enemy destroyers there, too, one of which blew up. In the words of the official Admiralty communique; H.M.S. *Hardy* later engaged three large destroyers. The bridge of the *Hardy* was hit and reduced to a shambles, and Captain Warburton-Lee was mortally wounded.

The odds were against Warburton-Lee from the beginning, but he had not complained. His duty was done.

2

GERARD BROADMEAD ROOPE

BEFORE the battle of Narvik, Lieutenant-Commander Gerard Broadmead Roope won his V.C. But the story of H.M.S. *Glowworm* only came to light five years later. Thus although the epic action was in fact the first naval engagement of the war to result in recognition by a Victoria Cross, the actual award came as one of the last of the war, instead of the first.

Glowworm (1345 tons) was one of the destroyers playing a part in the self-same operation as *Hardy* and her H-class consorts. Her fight occurred forty-eight hours earlier than the Narvik epic.

The last *Hardy* heard of *Glowworm* before her own battles was when the G-class destroyer was escorting the battle-cruiser *Renown*. During April 7, a man was washed overboard in the heavy flow of the North Sea. The weather worsened hourly, and in her efforts to find him, she lost touch with the main British force. With the weather becoming increasingly impossible, Roope, as commanding officer of *Glowworm*, reduced speed to eight knots. Then her gyro compass failed and she had to steer by magnetic compass.

Daybreak, April 8, 1940, saw her trying to rendezvous with another force in the operation. But she was never to find that force.

Suddenly *Glowworm* sighted an unidentified destroyer.

Immediately the British ship challenged her. The reply came back that she was Swedish. Then she opened fire. Thirty seconds later, still in seas as savage as any the oceans over, *Glowworm* sighted a second destroyer, and there began a gallant fight against odds.

The battle rapidly developed into a slamming match, with all three destroyers manœuvring at full speed despite the sea—and firing with all guns. The sea began to take a toll, before the enemy did. Soon, *Glowworm*'s director control tower was flooded out by the raging seas, which were hurling the ship about. Two men went overboard, and several were injured by the relentless rolling. But they scored a hit on the leading enemy destroyer. *Glowworm* escaped being hit, although she continued on the attack all the time. Then came a brief respite.

The Germans broke off the action, although already outnumbering *Glowworm* two to one. They were obviously trying to tempt her on to something more powerful. Roope knew this, but decided it was his duty to follow them to find out what big ships the Germans had at sea. He hoped to shadow them and report their movements, since this could provide vital information for British forces throughout the North Sea and Norway areas, in view of the impending operation.

Glowworm sailed on. A few minutes later, the German heavy cruiser *Admiral Hipper* hove in sight. The *Hipper*, 10,000 tons against the *Glowworm*'s 1345. The *Hipper*, with eight 8-inch, twelve 4·1-inch, and twelve 37 mm. guns against the destroyer's four 4·7-inch guns. Weather conditions made shadowing out of the question—and from that moment on all those aboard the *Glowworm* knew what her fate, and perhaps their own, would be.

Roope's one aim now was to inflict as much damage as possible on the enemy before being sunk. It was as certain as that. The battle began.

Long before *Glowworm's* guns were within range, the *Hipper* poured 8-inch shells at the destroyer, hitting her mercilessly, like a heavyweight matched against a lightweight.

Glowworm was game. She made smoke to avoid the attack, and then began to close with the cruiser. The second she was within range, Lieutenant Robert Ramsay fired her torpedoes.

Meanwhile, the destroyer began to blaze. One of her four guns was already out of action. Her range-finder was hit, her speed reduced. Then the upper yard of her mast collapsed across the siren wires. Her sirens screeched unheeded in the blaze of battle.

Roope realized nothing could be gained by prolonging the fight at this range. Then it was that he decided to ram the *Admiral Hipper*. Going in under a storm of fire from all *Hipper's* guns, and the terrible staccato sound of machine guns, he steered straight for the starboard side. A ghastly crunch signified the destroyer's bows crumpling against the cruiser's armour plating. Men fell to the deck in a welter of water, blood, flame, and smoke. Some staggered up again. Others did not.

Roope managed to draw *Glowworm* to four hundred yards away from the cruiser and then opened fire once more. He scored a hit.

But the *Glowworm's* bows were badly stove in. A shell passed through the wheelhouse. Another burst right in the transmitting station, killing most of the crew and all the staff of the wireless office on the spot. A third entered the ship under the torpedo tubes, crossed the whole width of the vessel, and burst against the forward bulkhead of the Captain's cabin. At the time, the cabin was being used as a first-aid station.

The same shell made a huge hole in the ship's side abreast the engine room. Another wrecked the after superstructure. Roope, so far, was unhurt. As *Glowworm* heeled over to starboard, he gave the order: "Abandon ship."

Ramsay was with him on the bridge.

"Go and get some timber and anything else that floats," he shouted to Ramsay above the noise all around them.

Hardly any one seemed to be unwounded. Ramsay helped heave the timber over for people to cling to in the water—if they ever got there. Lifebelts were put on the injured in the hope that they would float.

Roope came down. He was the only other survivor from the bridge besides Ramsay. Engine Room Artificer Gregg rushed up to them.

"I've been down to the boiler room and let off steam, sir, so there'll be no explosion."

"Good, Gregg."

As they scrambled overboard the *Glowworm* capsized. She floated bottom up for a few moments, and then sank.

Ramsay swam clear. He was conscious of dots of men, heads and shoulders encircled in lifebelts, groping, struggling; and others splashing, moaning . . .

The *Admiral Hipper* stopped engines, put out a boat, and picked up survivors; but Roope was not among them, though he had been seen in the water.

Ramsay was taken before the Captain, who told him that the ramming had damaged one set of *Hipper*'s torpedo tubes, flooded two compartments, and put her fresh water system out of commission. The prisoners were taken to Trondheim, but then the *Hipper* had to go to Germany for repairs in dry dock.

Only thirty-one out of the complement of 149 survived. Roope and 117 others died in an ice-cold sea.

3

NAMSOS in Norway was the setting for the V.C. to follow
Warburton-Lee's.

The campaign in Norway was not one of our successes
of the war, and the Navy was called in to evacuate troops
from several points, of which Namsos was one. Lieutenant
Richard Been Stannard, R.N.R., commanded H.M.
Trawler *Arab*. A merchant seaman, he wore the interwoven gold rings of the Royal Naval Reserve on the arm
of his jacket: rings dulled by endless exposure to the
elements.

It was late in April 1940 when he took *Arab* towards
Namsos. Somehow, together with other ships, he had to
secure sufficient standing there to be able to take as many
troops away as possible. A few weeks afterwards he would
be doing the same thing at Dunkirk. But, in his own words,
Dunkirk "was a picnic compared to the hell of Namsos."

Memories are mixed about those five days of continuous
fighting, but the order in which things happened is really
unimportant. The main thing to remember is that they
did happen—and somehow Stannard survived.

He took *Arab* into the harbour amid a hail of gunfire
from field guns and aircraft. Through his glasses he picked
out the fleeting forms of British uniforms ashore.

Even as *Arab* steamed in, enemy bombers pounded the

wharf area with high explosive and set off many tons of hand grenades which were stored there. Stannard could see that this wharf was the only suitable landing-stage, so he ran *Arab*'s bows right in against it.

There being no water-supply from the shore, he sent all but two of his crew aft in the *Arab* for safety from the leaping flames. With two volunteers, Stannard streamed the ship's hoses on the blaze from the forecastle. For two hours they fought the flames, but the task was too much for them.

Then he ordered the ship astern, and navigated her round to the far side of the wharf, which still burned. From this point just below the pier, *Arab* could take on troops. The incessant air attacks were telling on them. Just as the first few got on board, the pier began to creak, give way, and cave in. For the second time, Stannard ordered steam—to ram the collapsing underframe and so support the pier with the trawler's bows. In this way he got more of the men away.

Next Stannard turned his attention to the other ships. He fired on enemy planes which were trying to pinion them in one place in the harbour and sink them. *Arab* received a direct hit, but sailed on unperturbed.

Dive bombers took up the attack. One screeched down, and a line of livid bullets tore towards the ship. Stannard had his hands on the bridge. The bullets rattled against the metal bulwarks and one ripped into his right hand. He wrapped a handkerchief round it and kept up the fight.

Realizing that he must get some sort of base, as soon as an attack abated, he swung *Arab* away as fast as her damaged state would allow. He put her under a cliff-face for shelter and landed the crew and those of two other trawlers whose task was the same as *Arab*'s. Here he established an armed camp, more secure than a ship floating around in mid-harbour, a sitting target from the air. The cliff gave them some protection from the bombers, who dared not fly too near it, and yet they could direct their own guns at the planes—and perhaps shoot some down. This plan was imperative, for it looked as if the affair would last several days, and men could not go on fighting and manning guns without sleep. Here, those off-duty could actually sleep while the rest went on with the job. They attacked every enemy aircraft which was seen during the day, and kept a careful watch for submarines by night.

A day or two later, with their work still unfinished, the look-out saw some British soldiers beyond the cliffs. The planes would be due in to attack any time, and all the while the enemy's ground forces were firing at the retreating troops. So Stannard had the ship's anti-aircraft guns dismantled and installed in positions along the cliff to cover the soldiers as they withdrew to the comparative safety of the ship.

The armed camp ashore, under the lee of the cliff, and the Lewis gun position were repeatedly machine-gunned during the days they spent there. Bombers, too, did their best to drop their loads on them, but the position had been so well sited that only one man was wounded all the time the *Arab*'s crew and those of the other trawlers remained ashore.

Thirty-one individual bombing attacks the post survived. They came with sickening regularity. While the ship was there, Stannard saw a batch of Sherwood Foresters—he could tell them by their distinctive uniforms—completely wiped out before his eyes, as he scanned the far shore through binoculars; but there was nothing he could do.

Then as another little group of men staggered from the cliff toward the armed post, dragging their wounded with them, the German planes dived once more and strafed the scene with machine guns.

At last no more troops came, and *Arab* sailed into the

CAPTAIN B. A. W.
WARBURTON-LEE,
V.C., R.N.

LIEUTENANT-
COMMANDER
G. B. ROOPE,
V.C., R.N.

LIEUTENANT R. B.
STANNARD, V.C.,
D.S.O., R.D., R.N.R.

LEADING SEAMAN
J. F. MANTLE, V.C.

CAPTAIN E. S.
FOGARTY FEGEN,
V.C., R.N.

PETTY OFFICER
A. E. SEPHTON, V.C.

Imperial War Museum

LIEUTENANT-
COMMANDER
M. D. WANKLYN,
V.C., D.S.O. AND
2 BARS, R.N.

LIEUTENANT-
COMMANDER
E. ESMONDE, V.C.,
D.S.O., R.N.

TEMPORARY
LIEUTENANT
T. WILKINSON,
V.C., R.N.R.

LIEUTENANT P. S. W.
ROBERTS, V.C.,
D.S.C., R.N.

PETTY OFFICER
T. W. GOULD, V.C.

COMMANDER A. C.
MIERS, V.C., D.S.O.
AND BAR, R.N.

Imperial War Museum

harbour again. Stannard had frostbite in his feet by now, through exposure during the five days' ordeal: for this was Norway, near the Arctic Circle. As *Arab* moved out, one of the other vessels received a hit from a bomb and caught fire. She blazed fiercely, and Stannard knew it could not be long before she exploded. But he took *Arab* alongside, called for a couple of volunteers to go aboard the burning ship, and leapt across. They did what they could to rescue the crew still aboard, and when they could manage no more, they returned to *Arab*. The flames were jumping across, too, and it would be only a matter of moments before the explosion occurred. Stannard could guess this by the state of the fire. He cut *Arab* free. The burning ship drifted less than a hundred yards, then a huge explosion heralded the end of her.

He set course for home, with many precious lives in his charge. But the fight was not yet finished. As he left the fiord a German bomber veered on to the scene and signalled him to steer east or be sunk. An ironic moment, if he were to have lived through the last five days only to go down now as he was so near to escape.

Stannard ignored the order. He kept to his course.

"Hold your fire," he told the gunnery officer.

A tense few seconds followed. The crew and soldiers all peered cautiously out as the plane swooped down towards *Arab*. It was still a mile off. Three-quarters. A thousand yards. Eight hundred.

"Fire."

The first burst brought it spinning down into the sea near the course Stannard had set. Thereafter nothing stopped him. He put on full steam. *Arab* responded wonderfully and reached England so that the tale could be told.

So it was that Stannard won his V.C. He came from a seafaring family, which perhaps is part of the reason for his skill and daring. His father was a Captain and his two brothers also served at sea.

On the first anniversary of the outbreak of war, September 3, 1940, Stannard stood in the quadrangle of Buckingham Palace ready to receive the V.C.—which was bestowed on him as an air raid warning was in progress. It became known then that at school he had been called Dick the Devil!

But the war had a habit of demanding everything a man could give. Stannard could not stop just because he had won the highest honour. He rescued more of our troops at Dunkirk. Then he went on the Atlantic convoy route, the ocean where the U-boats sank ships almost every day, where men were drowned in icy water in the middle of the night.

For two years, Stannard served here. Then came one of the greatest Atlantic convoy battles. At least three U-boats were destroyed in a seventy-two-hour spell in March 1943, and others must have been damaged. The convoy suffered, too, but Stannard survived. It was a pitched battle between a U-boat pack hunting British, American, and Fighting French ships. R.A.F. Liberators and Sunderlands helped in the fight.

Stannard was sailing on his first voyage as captain of the twenty-five-year-old British destroyer *Vimy*. A U-boat was sighted at seven miles range early in the morning by an ex-U.S. destroyer, H.M.S. *Beverley*. She stalked the enemy till she got within two and a half miles. At the same time *Vimy* was called into the affair.

The U-boat dived quickly, but *Vimy* picked up her position on the echo-sounder. The *Beverley* circled, penning the enemy in a certain radius. *Vimy* attacked with depth charges. Her third attack brought the U-boat rearing up to the surface, her bows plunging out of the water.

She surfaced squarely between both destroyers. They

opened fire. The U-boat crew clambered out through the conning tower and just fell into the water in desperation. The ships stopped firing, and the men swam away frantically. Almost before they were clear the U-boat gave a great lurch and sank stern first at a steep angle—until only her bow could be seen breaking the line of the choppy mid-Atlantic sea. For a few seconds it was poised, like a black cone, with the tip of its bow towards the sky. Then it quietly slipped out of sight, and another U-boat had attacked its last convoy.

Beverley hurried in to pick up prisoners. Stannard counted forty she had rescued.

"Damn it! Send a signal, yeoman. Say 'Don't be greedy. Leave me a few!' "

Vimy accounted for nine more—but four of them died and were duly buried at sea. Stannard saw more than his share of war.

This was the beginning of the battle which went on for three days and three nights.

The war was nearly at an end. Stannard was badly injured in a car crash in 1945. But he recovered, and to-day his work is once again on the sea—as Chief Officer of the 29,000-ton Orient liner *Orcades*.

4

JACK FOREMAN MANTLE

INDEPENDENCE Day, the Fourth of July, was a fitting date for a V.C. to be won—especially in 1940, the year when Britain struggled singlehanded.

Warburton-Lee's epic was twelve weeks old, immortalizing once more the proud name of Hardy, Nelson's captain colleague. Roope had died in April. Stannard survived. Now summer scorched in the sky over H.M.S. *Foylebank*. And out of that summer sky, out of the sun itself, enemy planes suddenly swooped on *Foylebank*.

There was the staccato sound of "Action Stations," then feet running up metal steps, and the deck echoing with ordered urgency. Seconds passed and a plane screamed down to dive-bomb the boat. The crew heard the whine of the bomb, the plop in the water, and the sound of spray spurting over the bows.

A second plane, and a third, took up the attack, flying towards *Foylebank*. Jack Mantle, acting leading seaman, swung his pom-pom on to the targets. It shook a series of small fire towards the plane.

Then the next plane screeched down at the ship. Mantle gripped his gun tighter. The repeated pom-pom bursts broke all round the plane.

A bomb dropped straight at the ship, hit the port side at deck level, and burst in a thousand pieces. Mantle was only a few feet off. His left leg was shattered, yet he dragged it back to the gun-post. Another plane dived and he fired the pom-pom again. His hair flapped down over his eyes; no longer was it brushed straight back from his forehead. He sweated with the heat, the pain, and the fight.

The aircraft veered, banking steeply, but only to regroup for a second assault. The leader throbbed down again, out of the sun. The ship's guns fired, hit and exploded the plane. A second followed. Mantle was still shooting.

Then another bomb burst by his pom-pom. He was wounded in a dozen places, but still kept on firing. As the third wave withdrew, his hands slipped to his side, and he fell by the gun.

The award was announced on September 3, the first anniversary of the outbreak of war. "For valiantly standing by his gun after his left leg had been shattered" the Victoria Cross was conferred posthumously on Jack Foreman Mantle, acting leading seaman, P/JX 139070. P stands for a Portsmouth rating. Britain's premier naval port is proud of him.

5

EDWARD STEPHEN FOGARTY FEGEN

To the life and death of Acting Captain Edward Stephen
Fogarty Fegen the name of the ship *Jervis Bay* is sufficient
testimony. Her story deserves to be retold as long as men
sail the seas.

Fegen's naval life started at Osborne, where he joined
as a cadet in September 1904. Yet his associations with
the sea went back deep into the nineteenth century. His
grandfather served as a naval officer, and he was the
younger son of Vice-Admiral F. F. Fegen, M.V.O., of
Ballinlonty, Tipperary. Fegen himself was born at
Chatham.

As a sub-lieutenant aboard H.M.S. *Amphion*, he experienced the excitement of war in 1914 before almost
anyone else, for only twenty-four hours after war was
declared, the *Amphion* struck a mine and sank. Fegen survived, and he lived through the four years that followed
aboard the *Faulkner*, as second in command of the *Mansfield*,
and as Commanding Officer of the torpedo-boat 26 and
the destroyers *Moy* and *Paladin*. He continued in command
of destroyers far beyond 1918, learning his seamanship the
only worthwhile way by years of service in the most
versatile ships of the British Navy. His lessons were being
well learned. He was awarded the Lloyd's Medal for going
alongside a burning oiler and taking off her crew: a finer
feat than it sounds.

From 1924 to 1926 he found himself ashore at one of the three premier naval bases—Devonport. Here, he was attached to the *Colossus*, a training ship for boys. Then followed an eighteen-month spell in which he commanded the *Forres* and instructing cadets at Dartmouth. These took Fegen to midsummer, 1926, when he was promoted commander.

By a turn of fate his next port of call proved to be in the Australian Navy as commander of the Naval College at Jervis Bay.

When Fegen left the college for the last time in 1929, he could not foresee that eleven years later he would once more be linked with the two words forming its name. But a decade of peace lay ahead of him as he moved on to his next ship, the cruiser H.M.S. *Suffolk*, in China waters.

Between the coast of China and the Philippines, a Dutch merchant ship, the *Hedwig*, went aground on the Patras Reef in rough seas. Fegen commanded the boats' crews which went some twenty-eight miles in very adverse conditions to rescue the crew of this ship, which earned him a life-saving medal from the vessel's own government and a commendation from the Admiralty.

Back he came to Chatham, on the staff of the Anti-Submarine School there, and then as the 'thirties progressed, he commanded the cruisers *Dauntless*, *Dragon*, and *Curlew* in reserve. Just before the war Fegen was executive officer to the cruiser *Emerald*.

When war came Fegen had greater scope for his abilities. He had an unerring instinct to do the right thing. His command was no more than a projection of his character. Moreover, he was always on the spot where decisions were due. Whether ships' boats were stove in or washed overboard in those months from September to March, he arrived on the scene first—somehow. In mid-Atlantic Fegen stood on the heaving deck of the *Emerald*, his breath caught at his throat, with scant regard for his own safety but much more for his men's. In March 1940 Fegen became a captain and was given command of the *Jervis Bay*.

Out in the Atlantic, Convoy H.X.84 sailed from the New World to the Old, with vital supplies for the war—petrol and food. Thirty-eight ships comprised the convoy. They sailed in nine columns, with H.M.S. *Jervis Bay* in the centre, and the commodore's ship, *Cornish City*, leading the fifth column. The *Jervis Bay* was an eighteen-year-old converted merchant liner. In her charge lay the protection of the thirty-eight ships. In fact, one was straggling as November 5 dawned. The day was fair and the sea calm for the time of year. Fegen was in his element as he shepherded the ships slowly, certainly, towards Britain. As he paced the bridge of the *Jervis Bay* he realized how inadequate were the armaments at his disposal, should the ship ever have to call on them. But the convoy came first: he never forgot that.

On October 23, the German pocket battleship *Admiral Scheer* left the port of Gdynia. As Fegen glanced at his calendar on the morning of November 5 and thought of the firework displays in his youth, the *Admiral Scheer* was at large in the Atlantic. And during that very morning she attacked the British ship *Mopan* about 52° N and 31° W in the North Atlantic—and quickly sank her. No distress message could be signalled, so sudden came the end. So other shipping sailed on oblivious. Morning turned to afternoon aboard the *Jervis Bay*. Midshipman Ronnie Butler scanned the seas, his young face lit fleetingly by a setting sun. Nothing disturbed the scene. A hawser groaned as the *Jervis Bay* rolled slightly. But before evening the sea calmed down completely. And the sun shone. Some of the crew had just finished tea: others were waiting for it.

The time 1650.

"Ship to port, sir, on the horizon," said the midshipman.

A simple statement, followed by its bearings. But in a flash Fegen realized the possible situation. He got his glasses on it.

"Sound 'Action Stations.' Enemy raider. Tell convoy to scatter and make smoke. Report position to Admiralty and repeat to *Cornish City*. Raider at bearing 328°; twelve miles distance; her course 208°; position 53° N and 32° W."

The continuous clang of the 'action stations' alarm shattered the silence.

Scheer was veering round ready for the attack, but did not get any nearer. A few precious minutes passed. The ships in the convoy put on full steam, and laid smoke screens. *Cornish City* was shelled, but not hit.

The first salvo came from a range of 17,000 yards—nine and a half miles. The convoy scattered rapidly, changing three dozen different directions. The *Scheer* could not catch all of them, nor did she even have the chance to try. Before she had time to fire again, Fegen too changed course—but straight in the direction of the *Scheer*, not away from her. The *Jervis Bay* of 14,164 tons steamed fast ahead.

Her seven 6-inch guns were completely outclassed by *Scheer*'s six 11-inch guns and eight 5·9-inch. But the convoy could escape. *Scheer* could not chase it while she was being attacked.

Jervis Bay closed in to the attack, getting between the *Scheer* and the convoy. A shell burst in the water near *Jervis Bay*. She returned the fire—but was still out of range, for *Scheer* had manœuvred to stay on the fringe of the merchantman's range. It was a one-sided fight.

The second salvo came nearer. One shell hit *Jervis Bay*, raking the bridge and hitting the height-finder; the whole bridge burned, and the forward steering gear went out of action. Fegen was hit, too—terribly wounded, with one arm almost off.

But his ship's guns kept firing, and they made one hit. He staggered aft to the second bridge, his arm drenched with blood. A.B. Lane, at one of the guns, saw him groping his way along. Then Lane's gun got a direct hit. An earsplitting crash and the whole gun and its crew were lifted bodily and hurled into the sea. Lane was the only one to escape.

Jervis Bay was holed below her water-line, and she blazed from bow to stern. Yet somehow men managed to keep going and her guns continued to fire. *Bay*'s engine room was the next to be hit, so no water could be got to tackle the fires. She began to list, slightly, then a little more.

Fegen was on the after-bridge now, trying to control the ship from there; but a shell struck this one, too, and it was shot away. The ship could only steam in a straight line. Then a second hit in the engine room stopped her once and for ever. Her guns could not be swung round towards the *Scheer*. The forward guns were out of action, and as the ship headed for the *Scheer* her aft guns could not bear on to the enemy. An hour had passed, the convoy sailed on. Danger came now from *Jervis Bay*'s own shells, likely to explode in the fire encircling her.

Ropes, cordite cases, and cordite itself lay about the deck, directly in the path of the flames. Fresh fires broke out among the debris, and the crew did their best to put them out by stamping on them. They threw burning wood and boxes overboard with their bare hands.

Jervis Bay listed more. The decks were awash now and the ship's flag had been shot away. Some one ran up the rigging amid the showers of shells and nailed a new white ensign to the mast.

Fegen somehow clutched a way to the main bridge. He was dying now.

"Abandon ship," he choked.

Another officer called out:

"Aye, aye, sir," and then hurried over to look at the lifeboats. Only one was left. *Jervis Bay* was settling by the stern.

Captain Sven Olander, skipper of a Swedish ship in the convoy which stayed behind the rest to watch the battle, trained his glasses towards the bridge of the *Jervis Bay*. He saw the ship slowly going down—and he saw Fegen standing on the shredded remnants of his ship, both arms limp at his sides.

Still the shells came from the *Scheer*, pouring at *Jervis Bay*. In clusters they came, five at a time. Only the ribs of the ship remained.

The crew piled into the lifeboat, but before it reached the water it was holed.

Middy Butler raced round to a man on the fo'castle who had not heard the order to abandon ship. He was standing there alone, with earphones over his head, continuing his duty. He laid the 'phones down calmly and walked to the life-rafts.

The whole superstructure of the ship was burning. Four life-rafts were still usable. The crew—nearly seventy of them—leapt on to the rafts. Though the ship was sinking fast now, the Germans gave them no mercy. The *Scheer* poured shrapnel at the survivors as they struggled on to the rafts. Practically every one of them was wounded.

Still it was Guy Fawkes Day, and still the shells rose like fireworks. The rafts floated clear of the ship. A few of the crew manned the lifeboat, but it would not take many.

So sank *Jervis Bay*, Fegen aboard her. Five minutes later the *Scheer* went after the convoy.

Sven Olander aboard his Swedish ship mustered all his hands on deck.

"Well? Is it to be full speed ahead and escape—or stay to pick up survivors?" All voted to stay.

"Good," the skipper said. "They did so well to save us, I wouldn't have liked to leave without trying to save them."

Back on the rectangular rafts, the numbing night was upon the men, the winter wind searing their skin and freezing their faces. The midshipman, Ronnie Butler, ripped off part of his clothes to bandage the injured. Two of the crew died on the rafts, but the Swedish ship returned to the scene on the still-rising sea and took off the men in the lifeboat.

It was 5 P.M. when the *Scheer* was first sighted; *Jervis Bay* had lasted till nearly eight. The Swedes manned the lifeboat and rowed over to two of the rafts, from which survivors were transferred, and then brought to the ship. When the Swedish sailors could not work the oars any longer, Olander brought his ship alongside the last two rafts and saved the rest.

Sixty-five of the *Jervis Bay*'s crew survived. Two-thirds of them were, in peace-time, members of the Merchant Service and had never been in battle before. Yet they had all stuck to their guns till the barrels no longer fired and the deck was at water level.

Even aboard the Swedish ship the wounded had to await attention, for she carried no doctor of her own, and the *Jervis Bay* surgeon was himself one of the wounded. Some one tended him, then he set about the job of attending to their wounds.

Although *Jervis Bay* and Fegen went down, their sacrifice could be translated into terms of ships and men saved from the *Scheer*. Of the thirty-seven ships in convoy H.X. 84 thirty-one reached port. Three of these actually returned to Canada, where, incidentally, the *Jervis Bay* survivors were landed.

Nevertheless, five precious vessels perished: *Beaverford*, *Fresno City*, *Kenbane Head*, *Maidan*, and *Trewellard*. The Swedish ship *Vingaland* weathered the *Scheer*'s storm, only to be sunk by enemy aircraft three days later. Thus the toll was six ships out of the convoy lost—plus the *Jervis Bay*. Without her heroic fight, few would have made port.

Still the story is incomplete. For one of the thirty-one to get across the Atlantic, with a lethal load of petrol, was the tanker *San Demetrio*. She was set on fire and abandoned. Thirty-six hours after the *Jervis Bay*'s battle, on the morning of November 7, one of her boat's crew rowed back, boarded her, put out the fire—within inches all the time of the 11,200 tons of petrol.

Then, steering only by wind and wake, the *San Demetrio* sighted the Irish coast six days later. A destroyer escorted her to the Clyde, where she delivered safely 11,000 tons of her cargo. It was an amazing adventure, second only to the *Jervis Bay*'s in its glory.

The *Scheer*'s attack disorganized all Atlantic convoys for twelve days, till the cycle was regained with H.X. 89 on the 17th. The very next day Captain Fegen was posthumously awarded the V.C.

Edward Stephen Fogarty Fegen was one of three brothers, who all became naval commanders. One of them summed up his last action: "It was the end he would have wished."

6

THE Mediterranean was the scene of many battles, of which perhaps the worst began on May 18, 1941. While Lieutenant-Commander Wanklyn was slipping his submarine *Upholder* quietly out of Malta towards Sicily—where he won the V.C. the following week—a tremendous fight suddenly began in the seas off Crete.

The British Hospital ship *Aba* suddenly sent an S.O.S. over her radio. Without waiting for further news, the cruisers *Coventry* and *Phoebe* steamed straight for the position given. En route, Nazi dive-bombers loomed out of nowhere, just as they had done over *Foylebank*.

The cruiser's anti-aircraft drill went into action. There was an exchange of bullets and bombs through thick, blackened air. Up in one of the gun-director towers, Petty Officer Sephton kept the *Coventry*'s fire on targets. He clenched his teeth as he thought of the *Aba*. The Nazis had attacked a hospital ship. Nothing was sacred. Sephton knew that the cruisers had to get through, and he was determined that the planes, which kept on coming, should be beaten off.

The tower was totally destroyed as two bullets spat into Sephton's body. Yet he kept standing at his post, his straight, thin face pale, his clothes dripping with blood.

The cruisers were winning, but he carried on with the routine in a dream. Though he was losing a lot of blood he had to hold on.

Sephton stayed at his post until he died.

7

WANKLYN was not only the first submariner to receive the V.C., but the greatest commander underwater of all time. In the sequence of this story he represents the first tangible turning from the defensive to the offensive in the war at sea—a point of departure from which three more V.C.s were won soon afterwards in the weird world of the submarine: by Lieutenant Peter Roberts and Petty Officer Gould, both of the *Thrasher*, and Captain Miers of the *Torbay*.

The achievements of David Wanklyn, Lieutenant-Commander, Royal Navy, and of H.M. Submarine *Upholder*, more than upheld the traditions of their service: they inscribed inspiration afresh for all who followed.

Wanklyn went to war in earnest, with the command of H.M. Submarine *Upholder*, based on Malta. The tall and lean man with the soft Scottish voice and clear eyes set sail on his first patrol—and the Wanklyn legend was launched at the start of 1941.

Before he had time to grow his later-to-be-famous black beard to contrast with his fairer hair, *Upholder* reported back to base that she had sunk an 8,000-ton supply ship. The vessel was escorted by an armed merchant cruiser. Wanklyn took no chances. He surfaced at night.

"Fire one," he called. His voice was always clear, yet

never raised. Then, "Fire two." And with the second torpedo the ship blew up before his eyes, lighting the night with a vivid, vehement burst. *Upholder* lay for a second on the surface of the Mediterranean, exposed by the explosion. Then Wanklyn dived, before the escort could counter attack.

Before steaming back to Malta, Wanklyn encountered another small convoy—and again attacked. Three supply ships had the protection of a destroyer this time. *Upholder* hit and probably sank the centre of the three ships. The sub. dropped in double quick tempo from periscope depth to within a fathom or two of the bottom. A fifteen-minute spell of depth charges served as *Upholder*'s initiation to undersea warfare. Imperturbability was the quality which Wanklyn said was most needed by submariners, and under this first fire from the enemy destroyer somewhere overhead he felt relieved and glad that no one showed the slightest sign of excitement or unrest.

Wanklyn possessed this quality, too, and added to it two others—resoluteness and relentlessness. He had a brilliant ability to know when to sit 'unperturbed' on the bottom and when and where to attack, relentlessly and with resolution. The man himself modestly brushed aside all personal credit for his control of the sub. He said that he would far rather have the ocean to dive into than have to live in a city and just wait for enemy aircraft to drop their bombs. But that was omitting to mention his remarkably perceptive powers of navigation.

Four further patrols; the beard became longer, and assumed the pointed character it possessed throughout the rest of an astonishing career.

On the sixth patrol, *Upholder* sighted a convoy of five supply ships escorted by four destroyers. Such an escort indicated that the ships must have been more than normally valuable. Wanklyn torpedoed the 7000-ton sup-

COMMANDER R. E. D.
RYDER, V.C., R.N.

LIEUTENANT·
COMMANDER
S. H. BEATTIE,
V.C., R.N.

ABLE SEAMAN W. A.
SAVAGE, V.C.

CAPTAIN F. T.
PETERS, V.C.,
D.S.O., D.S.C., R.N.

CAPTAIN R.
ST VINCENT SHERBROOKE,
V.C., D.S.O., R.N.

COMMANDER J. W.
LINTON, V.C.,
D.S.O., D.S.C., R.N.

LIEUTENANT
D. CAMERON,
V.C., R.N.R.

LIEUTENANT B. C. G.
PLACE, V.C.,
D.S.C., R.N.

CORPORAL T. P.
HUNTER, V.C., R.M.

LIEUTENANT I. E.
FRASER, V.C.,
D.S.C., R.N.R.

LEADING SEAMAN
J. J. MAGENNIS, V.C.

LIEUTENANT R. H.
GRAY, V.C., D.S.C.,
R.C.N.V.R.

Imperial War Museum

ply ship *Bainsizza* and a slightly smaller German vessel of the Fels line. Both sank. Then he damaged a third supply ship, also of about 7000 tons. One destroyer stayed behind as escort to the damaged ship, while the other two sped for safety from the unseen eye. Later the same day Wanklyn closed in and sank the ship. In one patrol he had scored three successes.

About this time, he won the D.S.O. "for skill and enterprise in successful submarine patrols." His Number One, Lieutenant Michael Lindsay Coulton Crawford, was awarded the D.S.C. Others in the crew won awards too.

So to the seventh patrol. The little sub. set off from Malta for the southern approaches to the Strait of Messina. The beginning of the patrol was singularly inauspicious. Less than a day after leaving harbour Number One came up to Wanklyn:

"One of the torpedoes has developed an air leak, sir— it'll have to be changed."

Space in any submarine is limited. In a small one like *Upholder* it is doubly so. To haul the offending torpedo free from its tube into a compartment already containing four more torpedoes, and then to reshuffle them around to be able to load one of the spares into the empty tube is quite a complicated evolution even in harbour. At sea, under patrol condition, it becomes an onerous operation. But it was done, by half-past four on the afternoon after leaving base.

During the first four days after entering the patrol area, three separate groups of coast-hugging vessels were the only sightings made, but their size was not sufficient to justify *Upholder* in publicizing her presence.

Then, on the evening of the fourth day, in one corner of the cramped control room an operator was rotating a dial and listening out for enemy ships. He concentrated on one bearing, and rapped out a report:

"Ships bearing Red 20."

Wanklyn stepped over and motioned with the palms of his hands for Tubby Crawford to take her up to periscope depth. Crawford took over the trim. The navigating officer prepared to do the plot, the torpedo officer took over the 'fruit machine' for calculating the relative positions of the ships and sub.

A sharp order or two from Crawford and the boat rose steadily. When it was nearly up to the depth when the top lens of the fully extended periscope would break surface, Wanklyn said in a level tone:

"Up periscope." A slight swishing sound and the periscope shot upwards. Wanklyn was ready for it and bent double to meet the eyepieces as they rose between his feet. A flick of his fingers and the periscope stopped dead just out of the water. The foam fell from the glass, and Wanklyn took a quick look around the sky for any aircraft, then he scanned the surface.

He concentrated on the bearing given—Red 20. Smoke on the horizon gave away the presence of a convoy of one escort, two tankers, and a supply ship. They were a long way off. But even so, he did not risk the trail of the periscope a second longer than necessary.

"Down periscope . . . fifty feet."

His hand reached for the buzzer. 'Action Stations' sounded.

Quick movements, though no noise or scramble, as men materialized out of thin air. Upholder put on full speed. It was time for another check, so Wanklyn nodded to Crawford once more. Tanks were blown. The sub. rose.

Despite the speed Wanklyn could not close to less than three and a half miles. He went on rapping out the details. Course, speed, bearing, range. A chap read off the bearing indicator whether it was port or starboard and worked out the range. Finally the torpedo officer set various dials on the

large box attached to the bulkhead. These were reflecting
the readings given to him. Then with the complete picture, he pulled a handle at the side—and the 'fruit
machine' co-ordinated all the settings to produce the one
vital 'torpedo firing angle.' This is the aim-off necessary to
allow for the time a torpedo takes to reach a moving target.

Wanklyn took her up once more. The periscope was set
at the firing angle. He waited for the target to come into
view. But by now the ships were almost invisible against
the coast. The horizon was dark and empty for a few
seconds. Then a 4000-ton tanker's bow came into the
sights. It began to pass the centre wire of the periscope.

"Stand by. . . . Fire."

Wanklyn discharged a first salvo of four torpedoes, but
the cap of one tube failed to open—so only three torpedoes left.

They felt a series of slight jolts as the three left the tubes.
Then the next order came quickly.

"Down periscope. Go deep."

Wanklyn had his eyes glued to his watch. From the
range—far more than normal—he could calculate to the
second how long it would be before the torpedoes would
cross the enemy's track. Only ten more seconds to go . . .
two more . . one . . . none. Must have missed, he thought.
Then there came the musical metallic ping of impact of
torpedo against hull, followed by the rumbling thunderous
explosion.

"Nice work, sir," Crawford whispered.

"Only one," Wanklyn replied.

Then the two others exploded on the shore beyond.
They knew that these could not have been hits on ships
as the range was wrong. Wanklyn had estimated the distance to the shore—4½ miles. The extra seconds' delay
accounted for the mile further the torpedoes had travelled.

But long before the ship was hit, or the torpedoes banged

on the beach, *Upholder* had dived. For from now on she became the hunted—not the hunter. Silence was golden. A spanner dropped might be disastrous, if it were picked up by the escort's asdic.

"Crunch."

The first depth charge dropped. Then the second and third. The petty officer telegraphist jotted them down in his log as casually as if he were writing his diary. The sub. shook. But after six charges the escort gave up, and *Upholder* retired southward to reload her tubes.

Meanwhile back at base in Malta, the short statement was received from *Upholder*:

"Asdic out of action."

This meant that from then on, *Upholder* was deaf when submerged; without her ears. The whispered sounds in the distance which gave the sub. timely warning of enemy movements overhead and of impending counter-attack would be totally unheard. Any noise heard by the naked ear would certainly be too close for comfort; especially that of a destroyer's propellers.

Wanklyn was sure he knew the route the enemy used southward from Sicily and, sure enough, on the third day after the comparatively routine engagement—on May 23 —in almost the same spot as before, he sighted a second convoy: two tankers and an escort vessel.

"This is going to set us a pretty problem, Tubby," he said. "The escort is turning back northwards now that they're through the Straits."

It seemed strange to be leaving a couple of tankers to the mercy of the Mediterranean just beyond the Straits of Messina if they were bound for Libya.

"I wonder if they're really going across, Tubby. The name and colours on their sides are confusing, to say the least. Take a look."

The French and Italian tricolours look very much alike

when viewed through a periscope at long range. Yet even if they were French their present position suggested that the enemy were employing the ships. One ship was distinctly named *Alberta*, while the other appeared to be Damieni. Wanklyn thumbed his way through reference books and finally found that *Alberta* was Italian.

"Going ahead, sir?" Crawford asked.

Wanklyn had thirty seconds left to make up his mind: to fire or not. He looked once more. The ships were both heavily laden. They steered a southerly course. And both their names bore a strong Italian flavour.

"They're up to no good, Tubby. We'll attack."

He fired three torpedoes. One of them hit the *Damieni*, which started to settle by the stern. *Alberta*, her companion, began a series of zigzags. Wanklyn sensed, and then saw, an aircraft. The escort returned at full speed dropping depth charges as she neared the scene.

"Dive deep" Wanklyn ordered. Again they were deaf and blind. Twenty-six depth charges—ash-cans as they were called—cracked and crashed around them, some dull and muffled. All the while Wanklyn could not know by listening gear or periscope what the escort might do next. The enemy escort kept up the counter-attack all afternoon. The ship sunk turned out to be a Vichy tanker, so Wanklyn had decided right.

Upholder patrolled the area for nearly another forty-eight hours, Then, knowing that they would be leaving that night, Wanklyn had a last look around the enemy's route. The gathering gloom of twilight appeared to the east beyond a heavy sea. The sun set on May 24, 1941. Wanklyn's watch showed 2020. Then the V.C. action suddenly started.

Wanklyn sighted an aircraft patrolling to the north: nothing else, but he held on for a few minutes longer. Still the swell took *Upholder* with it to and fro. Depth-keeping was difficult. The sub. 'pumped' up and down. The horizon seemed shadowy, indistinct, to the east—but blood-red, clear-cut to the west. And one moment the horizon would be startlingly close; the next, while she fell away in a trough, the swell raced by the top window of the periscope, blotting out everything except the darkening water.

Ten minutes passed. 2030.

Then, strongly silhouetted against the afterglow of sunset, Wanklyn sighted three large two-funnel transports tearing at top speed on a south-westerly course.

"Ships, Tubby, three of them."

Wanklyn thought in a flash: light failing so periscope practically useless; listening gear out of order; only two torpedoes left. For some reason, these did not deter him.

He may also have seen the top-masts of destroyers, but the swell made sighting more and more difficult each minute. He did not stop to see if the enemy were escorted or not. He was intent to close, as fast as he could. But he knew that ships such as these would not be proceeding alone. Light bad, sea bad, time short—and getting worse and shorter.

"They're liners, I should think, getting on for 20,000 tons. One's bigger than the rest." In fact they were troop transports, converted liners, sailing in a line at 20 knots for Africa. After four minutes of following them, they altered course conveniently towards *Upholder*. Seeing that all would be well, or at least that they were coming in his direction, Wanklyn took time for a fleeting spin round with the periscope.

"Here they are, Tubby. Four or five destroyers. Didn't see them before. They're screening the convoy. Only two torpedoes left and a target like this! Have to shorten the range. Don't know their speed sufficiently to go ahead yet."

He shortened the attack and brought the sub. round

towards the oncoming ships, looming in the last light of the day. He screwed up his eyes to make sure where they were and read off bearings on all of them. He estimated speeds again; checked direction; compared them to Upholder's; and then he changed course. This marked the start of the assault. He had to hit first time with one of the two torpedoes. An audacious attack by one 'deaf and blind' sub. on seven or eight big ships, four or five armed to their topmast and full of fatal ash-cans. They practically skated through the destroyer screen.

It was 2032 and dusk, with the periscope eye all but blind. He manœuvred *Upholder* into the precise position planned. The mile-off attack was no good, and surfacing would be suicide. So Wanklyn got the sub. right in among the enemy. He peered through the periscope, swivelled it slightly, and saw the first of the transports, then the second. He had no idea where the enemy escorts were. Yet five destroyers roamed at large, and the danger of being rammed remained in his mind.

At 2033, he said "Fire." The torpedoes slid out of the tubes, their back-lash shivering through the sub.

And then it happened. As the torpedoes left, Wanklyn saw a huge black V heading straight for the sub.—the bows of a destroyer thirty seconds off, and getting nearer each one.

"Crash dive." Then as an afterthought—"Deep."

Down, down, went Upholder, while Wanklyn counted off the seconds from the time the torpedoes left. Fifteen, thirty, forty-five seconds. One minute. Seventy-seven seconds—then two mild and inoffensive explosions. But the same short interval separated them as the firing of the torpedoes from the tubes. Wanklyn had hit the middle transport twice. They heard the bangs without the aid of their 'ears.'

About a hundred and fifty seconds passed. Then came the

first of the battering bursts of the depth charges. The lights flickered; shades splintered across the deck; men were caught off balance. *Upholder* twisted and turned. Wanklyn could only guess where the destroyers were; which way they headed. It was a lethal game of blind man's bluff on either side, except that the ships knew roughly where *Upholder* was wriggling, through their asdic sets. Down the depth charges came, nearly two a minute shattered the water around the sub.'s hull for hectic minutes on end. And all the while Wanklyn cocked his ears in the direction of the charges, estimated the positions of the attackers, and steered his sub. as far from them as he could. Even so, some ash-cans exploded close enough to break the bulbs. The whole area seemed as if it were being subjected to systematic depth charging. But miraculously, almost, Wanklyn dodged them all—by split-second navigation and course-changing of a high order. *Upholder* traced a crazy zig-zag at different depths.

Thirty-three charges came in nineteen minutes. Then they heard—without their 'ears'—the ominous, thunderous beat of propellers as the hunter hurried overhead. Nerve-shattering seconds passed that got worse and worse as the throb of the props grew louder, louder, till they were racing directly above the submarine. Every man in *Upholder* was sweating now. But the sound passed its climax. Then they heard the plop of the charges as they hit the water. The ash-cans were dropping, down into the depths. How near to *Upholder*? On the answer to this depended thirty-three lives. For if you hear propellers by ear, it is too late to try and escape—you are right below them.

Four final charges cracked the water. 'Thirty-seven charges in twenty minutes' was what the log entry read. The last quartet would have caused broken blood-vessels to anyone not steeled to such an ordeal. But it passed, and then there was silence.

Then after half an hour their nerves were challenged again. Even Crawford felt in a tensed-up frame of mind. A series of light tapping noises sounded like a sweep wire passing over the hull. The mystery was never solved, however, and eventually it stopped.

The next decision for Wanklyn was to choose between escape and the danger of using his motors at any speed. The engines gave away their position when the attackers came too close. So he stopped engines completely for an hour. Not a sound broke the stillness. Thirty-two men sat silent near the bed of the Mediterranean.

Wanklyn looked tired but happy having outwitted five destroyers.

"Serve some tea," he whispered, and Cookie pressed his messmates to mugs of hot tea and slices of cake—and the last of the fresh-fruit salad.

"Needn't have bothered about the hot water, Cookie, we're in it already!" a wag said.

By the time the meal was over, the enemy had evidently given up the hunt. It was 2200. Nothing could be heard. If ever anyone felt cut off from the rest of the world, *Upholder*'s company did on that day. They were in a static submarine with no listening gear, and it was night-time above. The world might just as well not have existed.

"Periscope depth," Wanklyn decided. He grabbed its handles eagerly. He scanned the horizon round three hundred and sixty degrees, but the periscope was practically useless at night.

"Stand by to surface" was the sign for a stifled cheer from the crew. They came up where the transport had gone down. There was nothing to be heard in the darkness as Wanklyn clambered on to the bridge, but the breeze blowing across the heaving waters wafted a strong smell of fuel oil. The moon came out from behind a cloud and lit fragments of wood, broken boats, and flotsam—all that remained above water of the 17,800-ton transport *Conte Rosso*.

"Strange to think, Tubby," Wanklyn said as they charged batteries on the surface and breathed in the oily night air, "that she's now lying on the bottom just below us. She might easily have touched us. Perhaps that was what the noise was. We might have been there, too, with a bit of bad luck."

"Thanks for getting us out of it," Crawford said simply.

They set sail for Malta, ninety-nine per cent. sure of having sunk the ship, Their certainty was confirmed a few days later by a lifeboat of a large ship being washed up bearing the name *Conte Rosso*.

The official communiqué described the action in superlative terms. "With the greatest courage, coolness and skill he brought *Upholder* clear of the enemy and back to harbour."

The amount of tonnage sunk by *Upholder* gradually grew and with it the legend. Then Wanklyn received his reward for the *Conte Rosso* episode. On December 11, 1941, seven months after the action, the Victoria Cross was bestowed upon him.

It was first announced on the 6 P.M. news bulletin. His wife Elspeth sat by the radio waiting to hear, for the second post that day had brought her a letter addressed from the London Submarine H.Q.

DEAR MRS WANKLYN,

I have been officially told that the Admiralty are sending a telegram to-day to your husband saying that H.M. the King has conferred the Victoria Cross on him in recognition of his most gallant action and successes in Upholder. I want to be among the first to congratulate you. Everybody in submarines will be equally delighted as I am for we knew better

than others the measure of his sustained courage and skill.
With all good wishes,

Yours sincerely,

MAX HORTON

P.S.—When I saw your husband some six weeks ago he was
looking very well and both he and his officers and men were
in splendid spirit.

The award underlined the words of the Prime Minister
in the House of Commons that same week: "Half, and
sometimes more, of everything—men, munitions, and fuel
—which the enemy sends to Africa, is sunk before it gets
there."

By the time the award had been announced, indeed,
Wanklyn's successes had risen remarkably. On *Upholder*'s
tenth patrol, an escorted supply ship, the 6000-ton *Laura C*
was sunk. The sub. survived nineteen depth charges.
Eleventh patrol: another supply ship sunk and seventeen
depth charges from the escorting destroyer. Probably sunk
on the same patrol was a Condottiere-class cruiser travelling at high speed with a second cruiser and two destroyers.
Two hits were secured and the cruiser almost certainly
sank.

Patrol number twelve brought more bags. A supply
ship; a tanker, the *Tarvisio*, in convoy; and a hit on a
6-inch cruiser. After the tanker exploded in a darkening
cloud of black, belching smoke, an accurate counter-
attack came from three escorting destroyers. *Upholder* survived her record number of depth charges—sixty.

The thirteenth patrol was unlucky; there was nothing
to report, but patrol number fourteen was eventful. Wanklyn's work was beginning to bear the stamp of the supreme
master: a relentless inevitability.

So to the epic attack on the *Neptunia* and *Oceania*.
About the middle of September 1941, our reconnaissance

aircraft spotted three large liners at Taranto. *Upholder*, *Unbeaten*, *Upright*, and *Ursula* sailed as soon as they could to a preconceived plan. They knew the rough route that these troop transports would take, so three of them took up a position at an angle across the enemy's expected line.

Early on, *Upholder* suffered a severe setback, which would have knocked off balance an officer less gifted than Wanklyn. The sub.'s gyro compass ceased to function altogether, leaving him to rely on the much less accurate magnetic compass. This put precise steering out of the question and increased the difficulties of any attack.

Unbeaten sighted the convoy at 0320, in the middle of the night, but they were steaming too fast for her to attack in time. *Unbeaten* made an immediate report to *Upholder* and chased off after the enemy.

Wanklyn received the report and had little to do but wait till they came in sight. The night still stayed dark, ideal for an attack on the surface. What was he waiting for? The *Neptunia*, *Oceania*, and *Vulcania*, escorted by six destroyers.

Upholder's First Lieutenant was on watch when they were sighted. In a flash, Wanklyn was on the bridge. He saw dimly the dark shapes against a dark horizon: an eerie, exciting moment. The sea was choppy. Wanklyn realized that the sub. was some way off the enemy's track. He closed at full throttle.

With torpedo tubes at the ready and his glasses glued to the murky masses on the starboard bow, Wanklyn raced in to try and intercept the three monsters. After penetrating the ring of escorting detroyers with consummate skill, he realized he would have to carry out the attack at a far longer range than he would wish; and more serious still, the submarine was still swaying wildly from side to side. It would have been a waste to fire a salvo of four under these conditions, for if he were wrong once through no fault of his own, the vital chance would be gone.

He drove on and on, and when he knew he could not get nearer than 5000 yards, decided finally to fire. *Upholder* still swung from side to side, as the helmsman had to correct the course each moment almost.

"Never get on the line of fire," Wanklyn shouted above the elements.

So as the sub. swung across the target he made split-second assessments. Through the glasses he saw *Oceania* in the lead with *Neptunia* overlapping along the line from the sub.

Upholder swung across the line, and Wanklyn fired. She swung back again, and he fired again. And a few seconds later, as she came on course for the third time, he fired once more. He was judging entirely by eye.

Through three miles of sea they had to travel, on a dark choppy night with aiming almost impossible. . . .

"Ready to dive, sir?" Number One called up to Wanklyn.

"Not quite, I want to see them hit first!"

In the end the First Lieutenant had to go aloft and persuade him it was high time they were diving! So she dived quickly and moved south.

The three torpedoes took over three minutes to reach the target area, so long was the range. Then, as *Upholder* gained depth, Wanklyn's watch became the focus. At the precise second planned, they heard three explosions. One hit on the *Oceania* and two on *Neptunia*.

Three out of three! It was a truly amazing achievement in the adverse circumstances.

The first torpedo tore into *Oceania*'s propellers. She was in no danger of sinking, so two destroyers dashed in to try to get her in tow. But exactly as they did so, the other torpedoes dug deep into *Neptunia* amidships, crippling her.

Soon it was certain that she would sink, although she could crawl along at five knots. The third transport fled for Tripoli.

Obviously it was only a matter of minutes for *Neptunia*. Finally she limped and listed to a stop—and sank. The destroyers around her collected the survivors, and swung back to *Oceania*.

But Wanklyn knew nothing of all this. The unaccustomed absence of any counter-attack satisfied him that the destroyers were too busy searching for survivors to worry about *Upholder*. Wanklyn tried to get in touch with *Unbeaten* for help in completing the conquest. But he could raise no reply. So at 0445 he said, "Stand by to surface. I'm going up to survey the situation."

Slowly, splashing as little as he could, Wanklyn brought the sub. up, among the enemy destroyers. It was still dark, yet a ghostly glimmer from the east lit enough for him to see one ship stopped, with a destroyer standing by, and another vessel making to westward. Wanklyn concentrated on the stationary *Oceania*.

He took *Upholder* down again and made off to the eastward while reloading his tubes, to get a good position up-sun from which to attack after sunrise. At half past six, the sun blazed just above the horizon. The submarine came up to periscope depth, and approached the *Oceania* with her attendant destroyer. Both boats lay stopped but drifting slowly.

Wanklyn got *Oceania* in his sights, and the periscope slowly picked its way nearer, nearer to the transport. He was just going to fire when he shouted:

"Good God, 45 feet."

He had suddenly sighted a second destroyer bows on only 100 yards away. Undeterred, Wanklyn took *Upholder* along at 45 feet—and ducked directly underneath the escort!

Then he realized that this delay, and the drift of the

target, would bring *Upholder* much too close to fire, so he altered depth again.

"80 feet."

Upholder went on under the transport, too, so as to come up to windward. Wanklyn looked through his periscope next at an ideal range of 2000 yards from *Oceania*. Two torpedoes hit her, and the ship sank in eight minutes. So Wanklyn, alone and unaided, had sunk two-thirds of this concentrated convoy.

While Wanklyn was making the final kill of *Oceania* the Commanding Officer of *Unbeaten*, an amazed man, was peering through his periscope not very far away. *Unbeaten* too had manœuvred into a good position up-sun to attack the enemy transport, and was only a matter of seconds from firing at her when the Commander saw two columns of water gush up from the other side of the ship and heard two obvious torpedo explosions. He could hardly believe his eyes as *Oceania* began to sink before he could attack her!

Patrol the seventeenth was another brilliant attack, made by moonlight only an hour or so after leaving Valetta harbour. It resulted in the sinking of a Perla-class U-boat and (next day but one) of two Aviere-class destroyers which formed part of an enemy convoy which had been smashed up by British surface forces the night after *Upholder* sank the U-boat. Wanklyn moved on to the scene soon after dawn. Three torpedoes sank two destroyers. Another torpedo aimed straight for a cruiser crazily wandered off its course only a couple of hundred yards from the ship.

On the twentieth patrol, *Upholder* became dogged by a series of setbacks. She attacked and damaged a tanker, but one torpedo, instead of running in the direction and plane aimed, spun to the bottom of the sea beneath *Upholder*, exploded with a shattering crack, and shook the sub. severely. *Upholder* surfaced and attacked with gunfire, but accurate fire from two Breda guns forced Wanklyn to dive. On this same patrol, when returning to Malta, *Upholder* encountered the U-boat, *St Bon*. The latter sighted *Upholder* first and also had the advantage of the light. *Upholder* dived, firing a torpedo unavailingly as she did so. After a series of startlingly brilliant turns, to achieve a good position, she rose to periscope depth, and sent her last torpedo speeding straight for the enemy. *St Bon* sank.

A bar to his D.S.O. came with the sinking of the U-boat *St Bon*. A second bar was added for the sinking of another U-boat, and a trawler by gunfire, on his twenty-third patrol.

In January 1942 the submarine captain asked Wanklyn if he would like to return to the United Kingdom. The lieutenant commander replied characteristically: "Thanks, but no. It's my ambition to sail back home in command of *Upholder*."

March came, and he was operating with his customary brilliance. He asked the captain if *Upholder* could remain on the station for a further two months so that the sub.'s bag could be increased. His request was refused, but the patrols continued.

On May 1 Mrs Wanklyn received a letter:

MADAM,

I am commanded by My Lords Commissioners of the Admiralty to inform you that the ship of which your husband, Lieutenant Commander Malcolm David Wanklyn, V.C., D.S.O., Royal Navy, is in command is seriously overdue and considered to have been lost, and that your husband has accordingly been reported as missing. No details are at present available concerning the presumed loss of the vessel, and some time may elapse before it becomes possible to come to a definite conclusion regarding your husband's fate.

Meanwhile, My Lords desire me to express to you their very deep sympathy in the grave anxiety which this news must cause you, and to assure you that any further information that can be secured will be immediately forwarded to you.

The letter ended with the request that Mrs Wanklyn should not let any of the circumstances surrounding her husband's disappearance be known. The loss of *Upholder* was not to be announced at that stage.

With Wanklyn were lost Lieutenant F. Ruck-Keene, R.N., Sub-Lieutenant J. H. Norman, R.N.V.R., and Sub-Lieutenant P. R. H. Allen, R.N., together with a crew of twenty-eight.

At length the loss was made known. After the formal text, the Admiralty took the unusual course of adding a tribute to *Upholder*.

It is seldom proper for their Lordships to draw distinction between different services rendered in the course of naval duty, but they take this opportunity of singling out those of H.M.S. *Upholder*, under the command of Lieutenant Commander Wanklyn, for special mention. She was long employed against enemy communications in the Central Mediterranean, and she became noted for the uniformly high quality of her services in that arduous and dangerous duty. Such was the standard of skill and daring that the ship and her officers and men became an inspiration not only to their own flotilla but to the fleet of which it was a part, and Malta, where for so long H.M.S. *Upholder* was based. The ship and her company are gone, but the example and the inspiration remain.

In the twenty-four successful patrols which this submarine had carried out in those waters she had built up a long record of success against the enemy, and of thirty-six attacks made, no fewer than twenty-three were successful. The *Upholder* sank:

3 U-boats
1 destroyer
1 armed trawler
15 enemy transports and supply ships
1 cruiser probably sunk
1 destroyer probably sunk

Upholder was gone. At the summer exhibition of the Royal Academy in 1943, David Wanklyn's portrait hung in honour. Officers of the submarine service had commissioned Harry Morley to paint it. The symbolic pose is against the top of the conning tower with the forward periscope up. Wanklyn's eyes are alight with anticipation. His hands hold a pair of field glasses ready to scan the distant horizons.

For three years and more his wife never knew the final fate. Then in November 1945 came a letter from H.M.S. *Dolphin*, Gosport, where Wanklyn's portrait hangs, telling her all that was learned of his twenty-fifth patrol.

Upholder sailed from Malta on April 6, 1942, for patrol in the Gulf of Tripoli. On April 11 she was met by H.M. Submarine *Unbeaten*. After that rendezvous nothing more was ever heard of her.

On April 14, *Urge*, which was patrolling in an area near *Upholder* heard prolonged depth charging. On April 18, the Italians claimed that one of their torpedo boats had sunk a submarine. The assumption is that this torpedo boat located *Upholder* on April 14 while she was stalking an enemy convoy—and sank her.

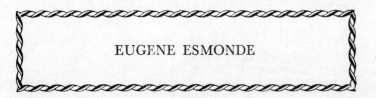

8

EUGENE ESMONDE

"His high courage and splendid resolution will live in the traditions of the Royal Navy, and remain for many generations a fine and stirring memory."

Lieutenant Commander Esmonde's mother read the words ending the Admiralty announcement of the Battle of the Channel. She looked out over the green and dark-brown landscape of Stillorgan, County Dublin. Still it was not spring.

Eugene had won the Victoria Cross.

She had lost Eugene.

Mixed memories of his thirty-three years moved before her. And memories of longer ago, of Eugene's great-uncle, Colonel Thomas Esmonde, who also won the V.C. He was one of the first to be awarded the decoration by Queen Victoria after the Crimean War in 1855, having served in the Royal Irish Regiment.

Eugene's mother, Mrs Eily Esmonde, sat by her window and saw the same sort of scene that the Esmondes had witnessed since they settled in Ireland in the eleventh century: nine hundred years of Irish blood.

She remembered her marriage to Dr John Esmonde, the three sons she had, and then in March 1909 the birth of her twins, Eugene and James.

Those distant days seemed for a second only yesterday

to Eily Esmonde, then they became aeons ago. She recollected and savoured the home on the Tipperary side of the thirty-mile lake. The sweep of the sea—for such it looked —and the Galway hills rising into the misty distances as the peat smoke of autumn wafted before them.

Then Mrs Esmonde remembered another day which was to stay with her always—when Eugene told her he had decided on a flying career. He sat for the entrance examination to Cranwell, but failed. He was advised to go up again and given a short service commission in the Royal Air Force. He joined a ship, and before he could sit a second time for the exam, they sailed to the Mediterranean.

Five years passed with the routine of the R.A.F. pilot. So his short service commission expired. Eugene was determined to go on flying, though, and he applied to Imperial Airways for a job. He became first officer on aircraft carrying mails by air between London and Glasgow, and other cities—an innovation back in 1933. The next year the routes became more exciting. He flew to Paris; took a train to Brindisi; and picked up a plane to Aden and Alexandria. Later, he flew farther afield, to Suez, the Middle East deserts, Karachi, and across India.

And still eastwards into the sun he flew. In 1935 he began a two-year spell for Imperial Airways flying a small plane up and down the Irrawaddy in Burma, between Mandalay and Rangoon. The trips continued till 1937, when one day the frail little aircraft quietly but finally collapsed right into the river, all but drowning Eugene and his passengers. They were rescued just in time, however, and he received a fresh assignment—which was to link him inexorably with the sea as well as the air. Imperial appointed him captain of one of their new flying boats which were to serve all points east. From Southampton, to Suez, Karachi—and Australia. The huge boats carried the first air mails to Australia. Eugene was one of the three pilots pioneering the air mail.

The world lay at his feet; a new, exciting earth. He saw Durban, Singapore, Darwin, East Africa, the whole wonder of the Orient. Peace still reigned from 1937 to 1939. From all towns great and small, Mrs Esmonde got letters and cards—by air.

Then, in the spring of 1939, the Royal Navy invited him to join the Fleet Air Arm with the rank of Lieutenant Commander. Eugene pondered. He felt sorry at the thought of leaving Imperial Airways, but decided he must. And he threw his energies and experience into the service of the wings of the navy.

He was commissioned to H.M.S. *Courageous*. She was torpedoed only days after war broke out; Eugene escaped. Next came a period at Lee-on-Solent and another air station in the south, where he trained pilots.

1940 passed. In the spring of 1941, Eugene and his twin brother James motored from Dublin to Drominagh. James was on leave from the Gold Coast. Eugene knew that he would soon be off once more aboard H.M.S. *Victorious*. At this time, April, 1941, he led a squadron of Swordfish aircraft on the carrier. And another of his brothers, Lieutenant-Commander John Esmonde, served in H.M.S. *Zulu*. Their paths were soon to cross in one of the most remarkable naval engagements of the war, in May 1941. But this was still April: spring in Ireland. A day to remember, sandwiched between thick slices of war which were Eugene's lot. For a day it were as if the twins had never been away from Drominagh. Mrs Esmonde smiled slightly as she dwelt on that day.

May now. A precious convoy sails well to the south of the Esmondes' beloved Ireland. Many miles away the German battleship *Bismarck*, with the *Prinz Eugen* as her scout, steam in their direction. But throughout May 24

British cruisers and the *Prince of Wales* shadowed the two ships. Admiral Tovey in *King George V* was also closing on the enemy. Admiralty threw in all they had got to try to catch them. *Rodney* was summoned to the scene. *Ramillies* and *Revenge*, too. Cruisers were guarding a break-out on another side, and a force under Admiral Somerville steamed at speed north from Gibraltar. The Germans sensed a net. Bismarck turned in her tracks to tackle her pursuers. But the brief encounter was made only to enable the *Prinz Eugen* to escape to Brest.

Eugene Esmonde comes into the action. Tovey sent the *Victorious* on ahead to launch an air attack with the aim of cutting the enemy's speed.

The *Victorious* had been commissioned only a short while. Some of the air crews had hardly any battle experience. She released her nine torpedo-carrying Swordfish into a biting head wind, raging rain and low cloud on a 120-mile flight. For two hours they struggled. Then late in the evening they found the *Bismarck*. Going in under ferocious fire, they scored a direct hit with a torpedo under the bridge.

But now it was night. An Atlantic night, void-black, and lashed with the rain, still. The squadron had scant experience of deck-landing in daylight. The captain of *Victorious* was very worried about their safe return—even if they located *Victorious* again. The homing beacon aboard had failed. Signal lamps were lit instead, and somehow all nine of the Swordfish staggered back to their base.

Eugene peered into the gloom and saw the pinpricks of light flickering through the rain. Surely he could never land there? White specks in a black ocean. He lost height. Still no sign of the carrier, just the lamps, closer now. How far off? Hard to tell. They could be bigger lights further off, or smaller lights nearer to him. All hit and miss in the chaotic conditions. Somehow he guided the Swordfish down to the deck. All still uncertainty. Then a bump. The nose lifted, dropped—and he was down. And so were they all. Into the wardroom, lights, a drink, and another world. Lights, but never could they be so friendly as the lamps burning up aloft along the flight deck which had brought them back to the ship.

The final chase, capture, and sinking of the *Bismarck* is history. But the other Esmonde, John, played a part, too. He was in the *Zulu*, one of Captain Vian's destroyers which were called in to help seal the *Bismarck*'s fate.

Eugene received the Distinguished Service Order.

First the *Courageous*. Then the *Victorious*. Next the *Ark Royal*. The first and third, fated ships. Eugene joined the *Ark Royal* in August 1941. Mrs Esmonde recalled the gap of three months without word of him.

Then that day during November. The voice over the B.B.C. "The Admiralty regrets to announce the loss of H.M.S. *Ark Royal*." Mrs Esmonde's heart stopped for a second. The news went on: "Of the large ship's company, only one man lost his life."

Gradually the story pieced itself together. Mortally hit a few miles from Gibraltar, the famous aircraft carrier struggled along in tow for nearly twelve hours. A torpedo had done its work well, though, and the vessel began to list badly. But by this time her Swordfish squadron had flown several sorties, carrying members of the crew to the safety of the Rock. A destroyer took off the rest of the 1600 ship's company. And before the flight deck tilted too much, the last Swordfish ever to take off from the carrier winged towards Gibraltar. Eugene took a last look down at her as he circled round and headed for safety. The *Courageous* and *Ark Royal*. What next, he wondered.

He returned to England for a review and march past of the Swordfish squadron at Lee on Solent in late November. On December 2, 1941, the Admiralty released the pictures of the last hours of *Ark Royal*, and another chapter in Eugene's crowded life was concluded.

It was all too recent history now. Only a few weeks earlier, before the battle of the Channel, Eugene spent nearly a month's leave with his mother. Throughout December he relived part of his youth at Drominagh and saw again at an age of thirty-two some of the scenes which were engraven in his memory through the intervening years while the world's images had moved before his eyes. Yes, it had been a long, long way back to Tipperary, from the pioneering peace days and the whirl of war. The lough lay still. The leafless trees traced stark shapes across the skyline. But indoors, the haven of home defeated the December landscape and gave Eugene a peace he had not known for more than two years.

Soon the December days fell from the calendar till Christmas had come and gone. And with it went Eugene Esmonde, back into battle. For the first six weeks of 1942, he lived at Lee on Solent and wrote home to his mother regularly. Personal letters, thanking her for his leave. No news of the war. She could only wait. His letters told her he was well. That was all that mattered. As long as he kept well and did his duty. She hoped both would be possible, but they were not.

Thursday, February 12, 1942, was a day of destiny for many men: the eighty-four ship's company of the converted river boat *Li Wo* and sixteen of the Fleet Air Arm. A hundred souls, few of whom survived. As Thomas Wilkinson, skipper of H.M. Ship *Li Wo*, received orders to sail from Singapore the following day, with his scratch crew, Lieutenant Commander (A) Eugene Esmonde had already taken off. Both won the V.C. within forty-eight hours of one another. Esmonde's action came quickly; Wilkinson's follows on February 14.

The day dawned. Esmonde awoke early. The year was

early, too—not yet spring. But blue-green sky lit the half-cloud over the Solent. The scene: the Fleet Air Arm's base at Lee on Solent, where before the war holidaymakers and casual visitors were often halted on the cliff-top road between Lee and Hillhead as a seaplane slid down the slipway right across the road and splashed and rocked into the summer sea. Planes were still a novelty in those days, the mid-thirties. Now it was 1942, and a different story.

Esmonde walked over to the wardroom to breakfast. Over on the airfield itself ground crews were already at work tuning up his Swordfish squadron. Esmonde ate breakfast and gazed out over the three-mile strip of water to the Isle of Wight, to Osborne and Cowes. The dark green woods and the light green fields dropping down right to the water's edge.

It looked liké a routine day. But no one could ever be sure. He knew that by now. His flying career had been marked by the unpredictable. It had been a distinguished career, too. He wore the ribbon of the D.S.O. on his navy-blue battle-dress jerkin.

A slight mist hung over the sea. Good day for ships to give planes the slip, he thought. The morning passed. He remembered Ireland and the leave he had just enjoyed.

Then a rating rushed up to Esmonde.

"Will you report to the Commander at once, sir, it's very urgent?"

Esmonde did not wait to return his salute, but ran out of the hangar up to the control tower.

"Orders from Admiralty, Esmonde, just come through. The *Scharnhorst* and *Gneisenau* are heading up-channel. And that's not all. They've got the *Prinz Eugen* with them and a couple of dozen or more surface craft as escorts. I'll get the positions and speeds worked out. Orders are for you to try to intercept them and attack before they reach the sandbanks north-east of Calais."

"I'll take six Swordfish. We'll be up in two or three minutes."

"I've already scrambled the crews. I'll come down and let you have last details in a few moments. Oh, and Esmonde—good luck."

The two German battleships desperately wanted to get back to the Baltic and the haven of a home port.

Eugene Esmonde, half a dozen aircraft, and sixteen men took off nearing 1000 hours plus a fighter escort. The Swordfish, fairly slow, torpedo-carrying planes heading for a force of some thirty-three German ships centred on the two notorious battle-cruisers. The Swordfish, six sitting targets for a hundred and more guns, flew into the channel of death. . . .

1005: Past Portsmouth and flying towards Calais to intercept. Over the water now, past the forts standing sure as protection against an enemy of olden days. Beyond the boom defence of the Great War. Hayling Island and the West Sussex coast receding now. Straight up-channel. No sign yet. Still half an hour to go. The weather clears. 1015. Suddenly a strong force of enemy fighters burst on to the scene. They rip through the Swordfish's fighter screen. Esmonde loses contact with all his fighters. The roar and whine of engines hurled about the sky. 1020. Machine-gun fire tears the fuselage of W 5984/825—Esmonde's plane. Others suffer likewise. They are banged off balance, but recover and fly on. All six are damaged. Getting worse now.

1030. Esmonde steers straight through the attack—and sights the ships. His plane is still leading. The targets sail towards the Straits. He knows now this is the end.

1032. The squadron is in V formation: 1, 2, 3. Esmonde is the spearhead. He puts his nose down. The plane comes in range. Shattering salvos spit up at him—and the others. His port wing cracks. Esmonde does not waver. He flies into the inferno of fire focusing on him from all sides. But before he can launch an attack, a shell hits him. It is all over in a split second. Fragments of plane hurtle down. Esmonde is blown clear—and killed.

The other five planes fly into the attack—stung by the sight of their leader. One after the other they dive direct at the *Scharnhorst* and *Gneisenau*. Torpedoes speed towards the ships. One hits.

And one after the other, the five are shot out of the sky. Down between Dover and Calais. Down to the inevitable. Sixteen men. None returned to the windswept runways of Lee. The guns of the battle-cruisers had done their job. An all-too-easy task.

Eugene Esmonde's body floated back to Britain, to the mouth of the River Medway. He is buried in the Catholic part of Gillingham cemetery.

9

THOMAS WILKINSON

FEW have heard of H.M. Ship *Li Wo*, a patrol vessel of about 1000 tons commanded by Temporary Lieutenant Thomas Wilkinson, Royal Naval Reserve.

Like Fegen of the *Jervis Bay*, Wilkinson came of seafaring stock. And like him, too, he was to serve in the Merchant Navy. He was born on August 1, 1898, and when he was just a boy of fourteen he joined his father's sailing sloop. During the War of 1914 he served in the s.s. *Alicinious*, a Blue Funnel Line vessel converted into a troopship. Four years after the armistice, he joined the Indo-China Steam Navigation Company. In 1936 he became a Master.

The *Li Wo* was launched at Hong Kong in 1938. She was designed for the Company as a river boat to sail the upper reaches of the Yangtse, but because of the Far Eastern war, it was decided that she should be confined to the Yangtse Delta, working from Shanghai. With her tall and sedate sides and fairly flat bottom, she was clearly a river boat first and last.

Thomas Wilkinson was appointed her skipper and under his command she sailed the waters at the mouth of the Yangtse for a year or so. When war broke out the Royal Navy took her over, and she became a ship of war—though all that this meant was the addition of a single

four-inch gun far forward, a couple of machine guns
mounted on the high sun deck, and a depth charge
thrower fixed at the stern. Her three-deck structure stayed,
decks that reached right to the rudder, where they curved
one over the other, and she still looked more like a ferry
boat, a river boat, a peaceful transport, than a man-of-war.
Those decks rose sheer, with no streamlining for extra
speed. She was never intended to need speed. High up on
the top sun deck hung two lifeboats, one to port, the other
starboard. The White Ensign fluttered now above this
deck. And *Li Wo* went to war.

Wilkinson became a temporary lieutenant, R.N.R. He
took her out of the sheltered waters of the Yangtse, into the
China Seas, and south to Singapore. On February 12,
1942, Singapore was a seething city. The harbour was
dive-bombed repeatedly by Japanese aircraft; shrapnel
and other scars marked the decks of the *Li Wo* as she lay
there at anchor. Then Wilkinson received the order to
make for Batavia. In the early hours of February 13, two
days before Singapore finally fell, Wilkinson took her
quietly out of harbour, with H.M.S. *Fuk Wo*, another
converted river boat, commanded by Lieutenant N. Cooke,
R.N.R.

The ship's company of *Li Wo* was eighty-four officers
and men, including one civilian. Mostly they were survivors from ships which had been sunk, but a few of them
came from army and air force units. Her armoury was
even less adequate, there being only a few dozen shells for
her 4-inch gun.

The *Li Wo* and *Fuk Wo* moved silently through the
before-dawn darkness of the Singapore Straits and anchored near the Raffles Light about 0500. They waited for
the first streaks of daylight before negotiating the Durian
Strait minefield to the south-west of the Straits.

In the afternoon Japanese bombers attacked, and their

relentless, high-level bombing scarred the ship. She beat all the attacks off, not without sustaining damage, and by teatime the assault finished.

After a conference, with the two ships anchored near a small island, Wilkinson and Cooke decided to steam full ahead through the night which was nearly upon them, and then anchor during the following day off Singkep till darkness dropped once more. That way they hoped to elude the enemy planes. Wilkinson put the plan into effect, knowing the odds against them were already heavy, but not yet overwhelming.

On February 14, 1942, two bombers discovered the hide-out, but the ships managed to drive them off again. Clearly it was no good trying to hide any longer. The two river boats—now far from the Yangtse and plying a peaceful trade—separated. Still before noon, they parted. Soon afterwards, about 1150, the *Li Wo* was sighted by a seaplane. Between 1200 and 1500 her hull and decks were damaged by very near misses from further air attacks. Still there was a chance, though.

Suddenly, at 1600 to the north-east a convoy of small ships loomed out of the sea haze. This was bad enough with only the 4-inch gun as protection. But then came a second convoy of fifteen ships, some of which were as large as 6,000 tons, escorted by Japanese naval units, including a cruiser and several destroyers.

The moment of decision had arrived. Thomas Wilkinson called his First Lieutenant, Temporary Sub Lieutenant Ronald George Gladstone Stanton, R.N.R.

"What about it?" Wilkinson asked. "Shall we go ahead?"

"I'm with you, sir," Stanton said quickly.

They called the scratch ship's company together and Wilkinson told them that rather than try to escape he had decided to engage the convoy and fight to the last in the hope of inflicting some damage. Wilkinson knew, they all knew, that destruction of the ship was certain and their lives liable to be forfeited within hours.

He took the decision to fight in the knowledge that, after all the attacks they had sustained so far, the total number of shells left for the 4-inch gun was—thirteen. The figure could hardly have been more symbolic.

About 1630 Wilkinson swung the ship round towards the enemy convoy. *Li Wo* hoisted her battle ensign and steamed straight for a transport some three times her size, which was four and a half miles off. The range of the nearest Jap destroyer was rather more, some seven miles.

Sub-Lieutenant Stanton volunteered to man the 4-inch gun, totally exposed as it was on the fore deck.

"I want some help with this," he called to the crew nearest him.

"Count me in, sir." The voice of Acting Petty Officer Arthur William Thompson came clear over the late afternoon air as the wake of the ship became wider and whiter with her increased speed. Thompson served as gun-layer coolly, effectively. Two officers besides Stanton, an Aussie stoker, and two able seamen completed the scratch gun crew.

Heading heedless of opposition right at the transport, *Li Wo* opened fire on the enemy. With the third shell from the little gun, a direct hit was scored, and the transport caught fire.

Still the *Li Wo* steamed in. The transport and three others of the convoy veered off abruptly, but the river boat was not to be defeated. Running the gauntlet of a hail of heavy calibre shells and machine-gun bullets, she pressed home her attack. Wilkinson meant to sink at least one of the enemy before his own flags were lowered. *Li Wo*'s two machine guns, firing from near the funnel, on the sun deck, returned all the fire they got.

The transport blazed badly. Wilkinson glanced down at his wrist-watch. Time was running out fast for the genial skipper. He was not smiling now. It was 1745. Minutes mattered. Before anything final happened to *Li Wo*, he had to make sure of the transport. For already the river boat was critically damaged.

"I'm going to ram her," he told the coxswain. No other way could he be sure. The bows of the *Li Wo* turned towards the midships of the transport. Stanton and his men still stood by the gun only a few feet from the bows. Nearer, nearer, loomed the larger ship. Fifty yards, forty, twenty, ten, five.

They met, metal grinding against metal. The transport was mortally hit. The crew abandoned her, and the next day she sank. But before that, long before, the end came to *Li Wo*. Wilkinson got the bows clear of the transport, leaving a gaping hole and dent, but by this time, nearly 1800, the cruiser had closed in. *Li Wo* had no ammunition left. A short salvo finished the fight. Her main steam pipe and steering gear were both shattered, corpses of the crew lay grotesquely across the decks. The ship drifted helplessly.

"Pipe abandon ship," Wilkinson ordered.

Rafts and wreckage supported those of the crew who still lived. One of the Japanese ships swung her machine guns round to the men struggling in the waters around the sinking ship. Bullets skimmed the surface, sending up tiny spurts, like stones thrown to skid over the water. The numbers of survivors dwindled: of a ship's company of eighty-four only ten got free from the ship.

At 1807 Wilkinson was still standing on the bridge. At 1808 the *Li Wo* sank silently from sight. The ten survivors reached land twenty miles from the point of the attack, but they were caught and made prisoners of war. Three of them died during the remaining years of the war. Only seven of the original eighty-four lived to tell the tale. Stanton was one of them. He received the Distinguished Service Order for fighting "with steadfast courage in the face of overwhelming odds." He still serves the Indo-China Steam Navigation Company as a master.

Nine awards were announced as well as Wilkinson's Victoria Cross, including two posthumous mentions in dispatches.

The little ship *Li Wo*, of only 1000 tons, lies at the bottom of an eastern ocean. But in the Imperial War Museum in London her scale model stands proud—as she was before she lived her last forty-eight hours out of Singapore: with broad streaks of camouflage down her sides and up to both the upper-deck bulwarks, with her anchor raised right at the bows, with her little companionway starting just above the waterline, with the Union Jack fluttering at her bows and the white ensign at the masthead. This is how she shall be remembered, as a little ship of peace which went to war and won the highest honour of all.

~~~~~~

10

PETER SCAWEN WATKINSON ROBERTS

THOMAS WILLIAM GOULD

~~~~~~

MID-FEBRUARY, 1942, proved to be a vintage period for valour. Esmonde's gallantry on the 12th and Wilkinson's final heroism of the 14th were followed forty-eight hours later by another action which won not one V.C. but two. As with Wanklyn of the *Upholder*, a submarine was the setting. In fact, at one stage of his service, Lieutenant Peter Scawen Watkinson Roberts spent a short while under Wanklyn's command.

Roberts was twenty-two when war broke out. Born on July 28, 1917, before the first war had ended, he went to two schools, Falconbury at Bexhill and King's School, Canterbury. He did not follow the pattern of Dartmouth into the Royal Navy, but joined as a special entry cadet when he was eighteen. Training in *Frobisher* was followed by his first appointment in 1936 as midshipman in H.M.S. *Shropshire*. Two years to the day after this, he was promoted acting sub-lieutenant, and on completion of the usual courses went to H.M.S. *Saltburn* in June 1939 as a sub-lieutenant.

War broke out. He wanted to get married, so joined submarines eight days after it was declared, "for the extra pay." That, anyway, is the reason he gives. Two months later, on November 16, 1939, he became a lieutenant, and three months later, in September 1939,

Roberts was aboard a submarine, preparing for action. This first sub. was the H.32, which was Wanklyn's first command. Roberts joined her at Portland as "commissioned office boy." He was still learning the drill of navigating officer. His office was no more than a compartment crammed with electrical machines and gadgets. To work out a course he had to sit astride one of them! The war was still only warming up at that time, and his main memories of the H.32 spell was the interminable drip on to the wardroom table through a leak in the fore hatch.

From H.32, Roberts moved to Harwich, where he carried out liaison duties with French submarines for a couple of months. Here, too, the war was not treated over-seriously—although the fall of France loomed round the corner. Six French subs. worked in conjunction with the R.N. Roberts went out on several patrols with them in the North Sea, and inexperienced as he still was, he found the *laissez-faire* aboard positively astounding compared to the rigidity of the Royal Navy. During daylight quite near the Norwegian coast, the submarine would surface nonchalantly—in full view of any intending attacker—while the captain took his dog for a stroll up and down the 'casing' or deck!

In this vulnerable position, too, the conning tower would be opened and hairdressing be the order of the day on the bridge, with the spring breeze blowing the Frenchmen's locks gently to and fro! When France fell, the blow to them was shattering.

Peter Roberts, softly spoken, with clear blue eyes, medium-fair hair, and medium height, had married in February, so took his bride up to the Clyde and joined his next sub., the *Tribune*, as torpedo and gunnery officer. Operating from the Holy Loch, they carried out patrols in the Bay of Biscay and off the north-west coast of Scotland. While on one of the latter, on the Rosemary

Bank, they picked up the sound of a U-boat on Asdic, and while both submarines were submerged, fired two torpedoes at depths of 38 and 44 feet. The Asdic recorded what sounded like a direct hit from one of these. *Tribune* surfaced and saw several signs of wreckage; some clothing floated on the water quite close.

Six months' patrolling from the Clyde, and then Roberts was commissioned to a brand-new vessel for the New Year on January 1, 1941. Three months' trials followed. But the blitz on Liverpool was at its height, and the Mersey had been mined extensively. For a week the *Thrasher* could not get out of harbour to do her steaming trials in the open sea. Finally she risked it and survived safely.

Mrs Roberts lived at Birkenhead for a month or two, until the submarine sailed up to the Clyde, where things were quieter, for her working-up trials. By a coincidence, the first day Roberts and his wife were at Dunoon, a bomb dropped at the back of the hotel where they stayed. From Dunoon came an exciting interlude. The ship was suddenly scheduled for three weeks' work at Loch Long, that well-named waterway north of the Clyde. They were due there next morning. Lieutenant J. Cowell, commanding, made a quick decision. To save the rigmarole of trains, buses, and sixty or seventy miles of Scottish travel at its most erratic, he sanctioned that all the wives, bags and baggage on the spot could come with them by sub. to Loch Long—and Arrochar at the head of the Loch. They sailed at the very dead of night. Three hours steaming and *Thrasher* was lying off Arrochar just before dawn. The torpedo range lay on one side of the loch and Arrochar Hotel on the other. Between them, water dropping sheer for several hundred feet. Beyond them, mountains rising equally sharply. Cowell locked the wives in one cabin. Now he was faced with the problem of getting them ashore without the Range Officer's knowledge—a senior officer who might be sticky about regulations! Somehow they were all smuggled ashore, like some illicit contraband, in the first light of an early-spring Sunday. Cowell had a good excuse for his decision to bring the wives along, though, for no trains ran into Arrochar on Sunday. Only two or three reached there on weekdays!

Thrasher's task at Arrochar was to test her newly fitted stern-firing torpedo tubes mounted amidships on the outside of the hull. After trials each day, down-loch a little where the water was deeper, the submarines would steam slowly back towards the range. So narrow was the loch— only a few hundred feet across—that her ripples sped to both banks and lapped against the shingle. And while she steamed back to base on the surface, Roberts and the others could call out to their wives in the garden of the hotel: "Be over about six tonight." A homely few weeks away from the war. But the spring passed.

Thrasher sailed down to Gibraltar. Then on to Malta, Italy, Alexandria, the islands of the Aegean, the North African coast off Benghazi.

Roberts got to know the lie of the land inside the sub. like the proverbial back of his hand. A bunk or a shelf was about all his own accommodation. The control room was directly beneath the conning tower and persicope—as always. Most of the forward space was taken up with the living accommodation, and right forward was the torpedo tackle. A long narrow passage was the main thoroughfare of the sub. Down one side lay the bunks. And opposite them, three "box" messes, one for the seamen, one for the petty officers, and a third for the officers. The 'wardroom' was a table, with seats on two sides and curtains on the other two. Abaft the control room came the wireless office, galley, engine room, motor room, and steering gear.

As well as having a normal First Lieutenant's duties, Roberts was second in command.

Off the North African coast they got some remarkable intelligence information about the strength and sailing times of enemy convoys in the area. About this time, Lieutenant H. S. Mackenzie took over the *Thrasher*'s command from Cowell. (Both are now captains.) One of *Thrasher*'s assignments was to try to find the limits of a minefield off the coast. By a bit of intricate steering and the 'ping' of the Asdic they were supposed to trace its perimeter, but somehow *Thrasher* got in the middle of the mines, an acutely dangerous position. However, by still more intricate steering, they extricated themselves.

Then came a cloak-and-dagger interlude before February 16 dawned. *Thrasher* picked up an agent, who had once been an official of Imperial Airways and looked on the Mediterranean as London do the Thames. They took him to Crete, dropped him offshore, and departed. The battle of Crete went badly just now. Several weeks later *Thrasher* received a signal to rendezvous at a certain beach at the south-west end of the island. Mackenzie and Roberts conferred. "Signal says our agent friend may have got hold of some Aussies who'll have to pull out of the island. We've got to be ready to take an indefinite number aboard."

"Sounds as if it's going to get a bit cramped," said Roberts, "not to mention stuffy."

The submarine steamed at periscope depth towards Crete. When darkness fell she surfaced. Roberts went aloft to look at the shore. From the dim outline of a monastery at the top of a towering cliff a light flickered. On, off, on. Then a break. On, off, on. Roberts made an answering flash with his torch—only twice: there were German gunposts on both sides of the bay. All seemed still, as water brushed lightly against the side of the sub.

"Have answered signal, sir," he said quietly down to Mackenzie.

"Right. Then we'll go in. Trim for'ard," the captain called. The vessel slid towards the shore. Her bows dipped and touched bottom. Engines stopped. For a moment nothing happened.

"What's happening up there, Peter?"

"As far as I can see, there are dozens of Aussies—and they all seem to have their girl friends with them!"

"Well, for God's sake let's get them aboard. This isn't the place for fond farewells."

A rope was hurled ashore. And slowly the soldiers were coaxed towards the sub., wading out with the aid of the rope. Seventy Aussies clambered through the conning tower, dripping, practically naked, before the *Thrasher* removed to safety.

Then she went back to the waters off Crete, and on February 16 followed several ships into Suda Bay. She fired torpedoes at a heavily escorted supply ship, which was almost certainly sunk. She spotted an enemy aircraft when she was at periscope depth and just diving. About 40 feet down the crew heard two loud 'clonks,' but they forgot them as the first of thirty-three depth charges fizzed down in the surrounding waters and rocked the sub. to its very bolts. At length the counter-attack ended. *Thrasher* remained submerged till night, then surfaced, still close to the enemy coast and in waters where anti-submarine patrols were active day and night. The crew always knew that the sub. might have to crash dive at any second while she was taking in fresh air and recharging batteries. As she came up to the surface, *Thrasher* began to roll.

"What do you think it is?" Roberts asked Mackenzie.

But before an answer could be given the two senior officers heard a loud 'clang' and a grating noise as of metal rubbing against metal.

"Sounds as if there's something up on deck causing it."

The conning tower was opened, and a rating reported a dark object rolling about on the casing (deck).

"Some one will have to go and take a look. The only thing it can be, I suppose, is a bomb from that blessed aircraft," Mackenzie said tautly.

The inevitable surge forward followed. All the crew within range rushed to volunteer.

"Now wait a minute."

"I'm the obvious one for this," Roberts got in. "You can't go," he added to Mackenzie.

"And I'll go with you, sir," Petty Officer Gould said quickly.

"Very well, you two," Mackenzie decided. "See what you can do, will you? But be careful."

Gould was second-coxwain in charge of the seamen on the upper deck, so he knew the shape of the sub. outside better than most of the others. He would have to soon, too, because the night was fairly black and they could not risk torches. He was also quite an old hand in submarines, having joined them five years previously.

Mackenzie tapped his fingers on the periscope below. He knew that apart from the hazards to the crew of a bomb exploding, the effect on Roberts and Gould would be fatal. More than this, if he had to crash-dive due to an enemy attack, he would have no alternative but to slam the conning tower shut and leave the two men on top—to drown; for every single second counted in a crash-dive. *They would be between the casing and the hull—trapped as the sub. dived, buried beneath an ever-growing volume of water pouring in through the perforations of the casing.*

Roberts got up on deck first. Gould followed. It was cold. They got their eyes used to the dark, but they could not waste too much time. Every minute was a danger not only to themselves, but the rest of the crew.

Peter Roberts saw the bomb. Then he saw a second. . . .

"Two of them to tackle, P.O. Better get a couple of empty sacks and a rope."

Gould reappeared with them.

The first bomb lay fairly accessible on the perforated metal platform which is the casing. They crouched low over it. Just then the sub. gave a lurch under the extra weight of the weapons and the bomb rolled from the port side of the casing over to starboard, where a rail stopped it. Between them they slipped the sacks underneath the bomb, and girdled it with the rope. Roberts eased past the bomb, then motioned the P.O. to do likewise. Roberts held the rope and handed a length of it to Gould. Together they dragged the bomb along the casing. Even on the sacks, it still seemed to grate and rub.

"How are you getting on?" Mackenzie called. "Tell me when you've got it to the stern and I'll send her full speed ahead."

Two hundred pounds of high explosive they pulled to the stern.

"Steady now. I'll shout *Now* when we're about to ditch it."

"Now."

Mackenzie sounded full speed ahead. The engines roared to life. A final heave and the bomb plopped into the water. No report. The sub. had steamed clear just in case, though.

The second bomb was a different proposition.

"Not going to be so easy, Gould," Roberts summed up after peering down at it.

The danger in dealing with it was going to be greater. It had penetrated the perforated casing and lay among the maze of pipes and torpedo tubes between the pressure hull and the casing. To reach it, Roberts and Gould had to wriggle a way through the hole the bomb had made in the metal grating. The torn metal edges scratched their clothes as they eased themselves through on their stomachs. Now they were really in cramped quarters—trapped beneath the mesh of metal that is the platform, with a live bomb for company.

Roberts did not recognize the type of bomb, so slipped his hand in his pocket and managed to get out a notebook and pencil. Gould shone a dimmed-out torch on the fuses of the bomb while Roberts wrote their details down shakily.

"Right. Now let's get on with shifting it." He stuffed the book back in his pocket. His elbow hit the deck.

Still on their stomachs, they set about removing the bomb. Gould worked his way round to the after side and pushed at it. Roberts pulled it from the forward side.

The gap it had torn through the casing was not really enough to let them get it out that way. The nearest exit was a grating some twenty feet from its present position. Between this spot and the grating lay various projections which could not have been better designed as obstacles. Very slowly Roberts pulled it.

Suddenly it emitted a loud twang. They both gasped. A sound like a broken spring trying to make a contact. This could be the reason why the bomb had not gone off, and why any moment it might.

Gould pushed it gently, Roberts pulled. Over a pipe it bumped. Again the twang, sounding loud on the middle-of-the-night air. Up top a seaman peered anxiously down and reported progress back to the Commanding Officer.

Another effort and the bomb moved another foot. For half an hour now they had been working, yet there was still seventeen feet to go to the grating, and still the bomb twanged. It was a bomb with big tail-fins, and it measured some three feet six inches, and like its companion weighed about a couple of hundred pounds.

They could not use a rope on this one: just their bare

hands, which slipped every so often round the smooth sides of the black metal bomb.

Roberts gripped the hull with his knees as he pulled it along. Gould got it almost lovingly in his hands. And all the while the wintry waters washed against the side of the ship. Still no moon shone; only the faintest glimmer of ghost light—and that broken by the casing above them.

"Not much further," Roberts whispered.

Three-quarters of an hour had passed since *Thrasher* surfaced. They got past the last obstacle.

"Right. Let's lift it now."

The seaman lent a hand from aloft, and in a minute they appeared through the grating, groping with the bomb. Soon it was up on the casing.

Roberts lifted himself up by his arms. Gould followed. The rest was easy. They rolled the bomb gently along the same way that the first one had gone. At the stern they gave the signal. The engines turned, the sub. shot ahead, the bomb dropped astern. They were safe. Roberts and Gould clanged a way back amidships; down the conningtower; into control. A slap on the back from Mackenzie for both of them.

"Come and have a drink, you two. You deserve a double, and you're going to get it."

Thrasher eventually got back to base. Peter Roberts went on a commanding officer's qualifying course, and on June 9, 1942, he heard that he had been awarded the V.C.

But the course did not go well. He had had only two and a half years in submarines, scarcely sufficient for a commanding officer. The day after the news of the V.C. came the anti-climax: he had failed his course and was out of submarines—a bitter blow at the time, especially to a man who had thought that what he did off Crete "wasn't very difficult."

But the war was being waged and there was no time for second chances.

11

ANTHONY CECIL CAPEL MIERS

ALONG with Wanklyn, Tomkinson, and Linton (whose story will be told later), Anthony Miers ranks as one of the four greatest submariners of the war: and he was a Commander, R.N., at the age of only thirty-five when he won the V.C.

In the early 1920's Tony Miers, as everyone calls him, went to one of the pleasantest preparatory schools in England. Stubbington is its name, and green playing fields adjoin the mellowed brick building. The village of Stubbington has changed little in the thirty intervening years: a few shops and an occasional bus or two. It lies a mile or more inland from the Solent, and some five miles from Portsmouth, home of the navy. So it is not surprising that many of the boys at Stubbington turned to the sea as their natural careers and lives. Miers did not enter Dartmouth direct from there, however, but spent some years at Wellington College before joining as a special entry cadet in 1924. As early as 1929, when he was only twenty-two, Miers specialized in submarines.

One incident ought to be recorded from his earlier days which shows him in a very human light—for not even V.C.s are perfect! After an exciting game in 1933, Miers, a lieutenant, entered into an argument with a petty officer who had also been playing. The cause of the affair neither could remember, but the outcome was that Miers attempted to strike his subordinate in the heat of the moment. Nothing came of it, however, and no one referred to the incident again, but it troubled Mier's conscience so much that he reported himself to his commanding officer and was duly court-martialled. In view of the fact that he had brought the whole matter to light quite voluntarily, he received comparatively lenient treatment. He was dismissed his ship, but soon received a fresh commission. It was never held against him by the Admiralty, and, as we shall see, he went on to attain great glory. Throughout his life, in fact, Tony Miers has been an individualist and a man with a powerful personality.

In command of H.M. Submarine *Torbay*, Miers won the D.S.O. and then a bar to it for his part in sinking eleven enemy ships in Mediterranean waters. On the very last day of 1941 he got his other half ring to become a full Commander.

The familiar pattern of patrols in the Med. and attack on supply ships went on and on.

Many times he admitted to feeling frightened while the ominous explosion of depth charges got nearer and louder to *Torbay*. Yet he never betrayed any emotion, nor did his crew, who counteracted each attack with depth charges by keeping the score of the number dropped on a board specially constructed for the purpose.

One day a torpedo had hit an enemy ship but not sunk her. Miers waited until nightfall when there was less likelihood of an enemy warship sighting the sub. on the surface. Then he came up, brought the *Torbay* alongside the strange ship in the middle of the night, and the crew prepared to board her. It seemed an eerie moment. Luckily there was no fighting, but as Miers stood on the bridge of the sub., waiting for his engineer officer to complete the task of placing charges to scuttle the ship, he thought of the exposed position all his men were in, and hoped they would be quick so that he could get them back to the 'safety' of several fathoms below the Mediterranean! Everyone else seemed to be enjoying the episode, however, and the cooks of the messes—officers', petty officers', and ratings' —eagerly hurried about the enemy vessel to replenish the sub.'s food stocks!

"Make a change from tinned bangers!" he heard one of the cooks call as they stumbled on some delicacy of Italian cuisine.

He breathed a sigh of real relief when the operation was over and his crew settled down again to the rigid routine of a submarine on patrol in wartime. Though it was all literally a matter of life and death, Miers managed to display a capacity for attracting deep affection from his men, and he seemed able to find the funnier side of life, even if he pretended not to be aware of it at the time.

The nearest *Torbay* came to disaster happened another night—one of the many spent among alien waters. While the sub. was on the surface re-charging her batteries, Miers was resting momentarily near the conning tower hatch, propped up against a pillow he took up on deck specially to support him.

Out of the night came the cry from the look-out:

"Destroyer astern, sir, heading straight for us."

"Crash dive," Miers said.

Action stations sounded. The men up top leapt below. All went to their posts. Miers was last to come. He pulled the conning tower hatch shut—but it stuck. It would not fit. Every second the enemy ship got nearer. He thought quickly. He tried the hatch again. Finally he jumped from the bridge right down to the control room at a single leap. The sub. was diving now. Still the hatch would not shut. Miers reached up, slammed shut the lower hatch just as the sub. submerged. They heard the splash and crash of

water pouring into the conning tower. But they were
down. Six feet. Twelve. The destroyer passed overhead.
A babble of noise now filled the control room: the hectic
throb of the enemy's propellers and the continuous ringing
of the diving klaxon bell which was short-circuited by the
water in the conning tower and just went on and on blaring
and blasting.

The first lieutenant struggled to shout orders to correct
the trim for all the extra water on board, and to add to the
confusion, depth charges shook and shuddered the submarine as she dived ever deeper down to the darkness of
the middle-of-the-night Mediterranean. Finally the klaxon
circuit seemed to tire of its incessant sound, and the depth
charges got fainter. All was peace once more.

The next time that the sub. surfaced water poured into
the control room from the conning tower. And when it
was baled out and the upper hatch was opened, it was
discovered, to the mortification of Commander Miers,
that it had been his pillow which had wedged itself firmly
at the rim of the conning tower hatch and had prevented
it from closing!

Patrolling at periscope depth on the third day of the
third month of 1942, he suddenly spotted a large convoy
on the horizon escorted by three Italian destroyers.

"All out of range," he announced curtly to Lieutenant
Hugh Kidd, who wore the ribbon of the D.S.O. for gallant
submarine service.

"I'm going to trail 'em," Miers decided. "May take
some time, but it should be worth while."

The Mediterranean day drew on. Miers took *Torbay*
along well behind the enemy convoy. Hours dragged
by.

"Land ahead," he said, after one of his periodic peeps
through the sub.'s 'eyes.'

"Looks like a harbour. Must be Corfu."

The convoy changed course slightly as the leading ship in the line reached the approach to the harbour.

"They're going in. We'll follow later. Can't catch them otherwise, and we're not coming all this way for nothing —don't you agree, Kidd?"

The two-ringer nodded from the depths of the electrical equipment.

The long convoy wound its way into port, the destroyers bringing up the rear, tucking the supply ships in safely, as it were.

Miers took *Torbay* towards the harbour entrance. He saw further warships at anchor inside the harbour.

"Not going to be easy," he decided.

He observed the route the ships took, noticing that the only way in was through a single narrow channel. If he went off course he risked grounding the sub. or else striking a mine.

With infinite care Miers guided his craft in slowly, slowly, along the channel. Through his periscope he could see the enemy ships getting slightly nearer. They were still a long way off, however, much too far to chance a torpedo with any high hope of recording a hit. No one spoke much in the sub. when she crept gradually into the heart of the harbour.

They were in, surrounded on three and a half sides by enemy territory—and enemy vessels. There were probably as many more again warships as the three escorting the convoy: half a dozen destroyers all within gun-range.

Delicately, so as not to disturb the surface of the water more than necessary, he glided the periscope up above sea level and scanned the scene. The sun had set, and the outlines of the ships were already becoming hazy in the March evening air. He would have to wait for next morning to make an attack, for the trip up-harbour had taken most of the afternoon and conditions were against a successful sub. assault.

Miers pulled the periscope down again and then took a walk beyond the control room along to the messes. He ran into Engine Room Artificer Pinch.

"Hello, Pinch. Bit of an awkward spot to spend the night, eh, under the water in some strange port? How long is it since you joined *Torbay*? You've got about the longest service in her, haven't you?"

"Two years ago this week, sir. March 1940, I first saw her, and we've been a few miles in her since, sir."

"We certainly have. Well, there's many a patrol to be done after this, so don't worry—we'll get back to base."

Miers wandered as far as he could, watching the ratings at rest and on watch. One read a book. Another wrote a letter home. (Miers wondered where he would post it.) A third sailor smiled at him as Miers passed his bunk.

The night wore on in quietness; the engines, which had never turned above slow once the sub. was in the harbour, had been stopped for hours.

Kidd came up to Miers.

"Some bad news, sir. We'll have to re-charge batteries. Never make it tomorrow out of here unless we do."

"Hmm." Miers said no more. He could try to take the sub. out of harbour now, of course, and surface in safety clear of the coast; but he preferred to stay.

"Right. Nothing for it, I suppose, but to take her up. I'll just take a look aloft first."

Miers screwed up his eyes to get them used to the darkness he expected to see through the periscope. What he saw gave him a shock. It was almost as light as day. A brilliant full moon shone over the water, streaking the harbour with quicksilver shafts.

"It's as bright as broad daylight," he said, then added, "Stand by to surface."

Unbelievably slowly, the sub. broke surface, the bows and the conning tower parting the wavelets in two places. She slid to a stop, and a duty rating eased the two hatches open to take in some fresh air. There on the surface, well within the foreign harbour, the sub. lay silhouetted for all to see; black as jet against the silver-grey sea.

"No talking. Nothing above a whisper," went the order.

Minutes ticked by. The batteries gained new life. The men sat around, still. The brass clock turned one revolution, then a second. Two hours *Torbay* had to stay surfaced. If just one look-out had spotted her she could not have escaped destruction; but no one did. The moon moved behind a cloud after the first hour, then came out again a minute or two later and the light seemed brighter than ever. They heard in the distance some sailors changing watch at the dead of night.

"How much longer?" Miers asked.

"Batteries charged," came back the welcome assurance.

"Well, let's get below again as quick as we can."

The hatches were closed carefully, quietly. The engines turned over scarcely above a murmur, the men breathed more freely, and the long metal craft vanished underwater as quietly and mysteriously as she had risen a couple of hours earlier.

Morning came.

"Periscope depth."

Miers grabbed the periscope eagerly and swung it round to get a look at the shipping in full daylight.

"Convoy all gone," he told the First Lieutenant, "but there are a couple of supply ships left over there, about 5000 tons each, I'd say, and one of the destroyers. The others seem to have flitted. Must have been after we submerged. Right. Stand by to attack."

The engines moved faster. The sub. swung forward now, full speed ahead. He pressed her home fairly close to the anchorages and on a swinging turn smacked a torpedo at each of the three ships in ultra-rapid succession. Her periscope traced an arc of white in the glassy-calm water. As the sub. completed her turn, or even earlier, both supply ships exploded amidships with a shattering sound.

Miers took the sub. down deep the moment the tubes had fired, and almost touched bottom. She lay there for half an hour. At that stage he did not know that he had sunk the two supply vessels and missed the destroyer.

He brought *Torbay* up to periscope depth—still right in the harbour—and ran right among some small boats all searching frantically for his sub. He crash-dived deep again as depth charges volleyed down after the sub. The crew kept count. Ten; twenty; forty. Miers made for the nearest exit from the harbour, in a very straight line. He was at periscope depth now to guide them through.

"Nearly at the end of the channel now," he reported. Then: "My God. Crash dive."

Into the periscope at the shortest possible range headed a patrol vessel, only yards from the sub.'s bow. For the second time the crash dive came off. He had thwarted the anti-submarine craft who were hovering all along the long exit channel—and also the continuous air patrols overhead.

It was mid-morning when Miers reached open water—seventeen hours after he had led the *Torbay* into the enemy enclosure.

A few months later, on July 28, 1942, a unique occasion occurred at Buckingham Palace. Commander Anthony Miers was invested with the V.C.; Lieutenants Kidd, Chapman, and Verschoyle-Campbell received a D.S.O. and two bars to the D.S.C.; and twenty-four ratings received D.S.M.s or bars to the D.S.M.

It was the first time that officers and men of one of H.M.

ships have been awarded their decorations at the same
investiture.

The story goes that the four officers were to have been
invested at one ceremony and the ratings at another.
Miers is quoted as having said that if they could not all
attend together, then he did not want his V.C. And so the
ship's company were not separated, but stayed united—as
they had been those long hours, and months, beneath the
Mediterranean.

12

ROBERT EDWARD DUDLEY RYDER
STEPHEN HALDEN BEATTIE
WILLIAM ALFRED SAVAGE

SUBMARINES stabbed the enemy from below the surface. Allied air forces were beginning the assault in earnest from up above. Nevertheless, in the spring of 1942 Britain had yet to swing over to the offensive. Singapore had fallen— and Thomas Wilkinson died. With the evacuation of Crete we had lost our last foothold in Europe; the Russians were still retreating; bombs scarred our cities; and through it all was waged the battle of the Atlantic.

Twelve V.C.s of a total of twenty-four had by this time been won. These dozen V.C.s reflected the pattern of the last two and a half years. The struggle of Norway; the *Jervis Bay* in the Atlantic; the submarines in the Mediterranean and elsewhere; the sinking of the *Bismarck*; the escape of the *Scharnhorst* and *Gneisenau* up the Channel; operations off Crete.

We were approaching the turning point, but as yet had not actually turned what Mr Churchill called "the hinge of fate." Things were still serious. We had to feel the full force of Rommel in Africa. With the evacuation of Singapore, the Japanese menace made itself more and more apparent. Pearl Harbour had been a blow to the United States; the sinking of the *Prince of Wales* and *Repulse* an equally heavy one for Britain.

So as a boost to morale alone, the need was for a feat

of arms somewhere—and soon: something to cheer the Allied cause, to show the world we were eventually going to win. For strategic reasons much more, however, the need came into being to launch the raid which was to set astir the blood of a Europe in bondage: the attack on St Nazaire.

When the 56,000-ton battleship *Bismarck* was sunk in May 1941 it subsequently became disclosed that she was heading for St Nazaire, the only port with a dock large enough to berth her. For the rest of 1941 the powerful enemy battle-cruisers, *Scharnhorst* and *Gneisenau*—together with the *Prinz Eugen*—waited at Brest, also on the west coast of France.

Early in 1942, however, a new battleship began to appear on the scene—the Norwegian scene. She was the *Tirpitz*, and she shifted restlessly round and about during January and February 1942. She had been completed only by this winter. She had with her the pocket battleships *Scheer* and *Lutzow* and heavy cruisers of the Hipper class. The possibility now existed of a powerful force erupting from Norwegian waters, joining forces with the other German units based on Brest, and causing chaos to Allied convoys. But to do this, the *Tirpitz* would need a port in the Bay of Biscay where any repairs or inevitable maintenance could be done. St Nazaire was the one port possible to take the *Tirpitz*. It could be berthed only in the Normandie Dock, built before the war to take the famous French liner.

Brest was a high priority on Bomber Command's list of objectives, but a target such as the Normandie Dock at St Nazaire could hardly be bombed sufficiently surely and heavily to render it useless.

By February 1942 Brest was no place for the famous trio *Scharnhorst*, *Gneisenau*, and *Prinz Eugen*. So on February 12, under cover of low visibility and a strong fighter support, they slipped out of the harbour, round the north coast of France and through the English Channel to Germany. And Eugene Esmonde died trying to stop them.

Despite this, St Nazaire remained as a dangerously efficient port, capable of catering for the *Tirpitz*. So a fortnight after the three German warships had eluded us, "Operation Chariot" was submitted to the Commander-in-Chief, Plymouth. By March 3 it had been approved, and on March 26 a great combined operation was launched.

But before this, much planning and preparation had to be executed. The overall idea was to damage the dock sufficiently to render it useless for the *Tirpitz*—or indeed any other ship. Other assaults would be made on additional objectives in the harbour region, but the first and foremost object of the attack would be the dock. To do this the lock gates or caisson at the outer, seaward end of the dock must be destroyed. These gates were 167 feet long, 54 feet tall, and 35 feet thick. Also at St Nazaire were shelter pens for German U-boats; these and various other targets were taken into consideration when formulating the plan of attack.

The core of the plan put forward was an unusual one—and one which met with much argument before being finally adopted. The lock gates were to be rammed and broken by an 'explosive destroyer.' An imaginative idea, this. It was originally suggested by Captain J. Hughes-Hallett, and that the project finally went forward was due considerably to the inspiration and energy of Vice-Admiral Lord Louis Mountbatten, recently appointed as Chief of Combined Operations—land, sea, and air.

The plan had to be carefully considered, as the Loire Estuary presented an approach to St Nazaire which was well covered with coastal batteries. These were placed intermittently along each side of the estuary. Once past a certain spot, however, a mile or so from the dock, the gates could be rushed. The main obstacles at this close range were batteries of high velocity guns, one on each bank—the left, or port, side which was the shore where St Nazaire lay, and the right, or starboard side. And, of course, there would be flak positions on the jetties, waterfront, and house-tops. A hot reception was in prospect.

Out to sea they expected to find a guard-ship anchored half a mile from the Old Mole, a promontory on the St Nazaire bank. All such hazards as minefields and under-water obstructions had to be ignored in preparing the plans. The garrison of the port might be as many as 10,000 men.

Impressive as all these defences sounded on paper, the attackers would have the advantage of surprise—up to a point—and of knowing exactly where the coastal guns were situated. Surprise was the key quality by which the success or otherwise of the raid would be measured. For an undetected approach past the heavier batteries was to be the aim, undetected until the short-range defences could be overwhelmed by the boat's own guns.

The plan as approved by the Chiefs of Staff took the form of an assault by one expendable explosive destroyer and a dozen Motor Launches carrying Commandos. The destroyer was to ram the outer gate of the dock at a suffi-cient speed to cut the torpedo net protecting it. While troops from the destroyer got ashore to attack the pumping house, flak positions, and a fuel dump, the destroyer would be prepared for scuttling and demolition.

While this was in progress, other landings were to be made at two points—the Old Mole, the promontory already mentioned, and the Old Entrance to the inner harbour installations, where some steps existed. These subsidiary landings were to disrupt the U-boat base generally, silence flak positions firing on our forces, and secure two small islands in the port area. One of these would be essential, as it was from the Ile de St Nazaire that the withdrawal was due—at the Old Mole.

The appointments made for the attack were as follows: Commander Robert Edward Dudley Ryder to be in charge of all naval forces, Lieutenant-Colonel A. C. Newman the military force commander, and Lieutenant-Commander Stephen Halden Beattie in command of the Ex-United States destroyer, *Campbeltown*. The ship was one of the fifty obsolete destroyers transferred to Britain a little time earlier, so would be no great loss.

Accommodation and organization proved scanty. Ryder had not even got a car, a staff, or headquarters, but they soon settled themselves into the conservatory of a hotel on the sea-front at Falmouth, a good jumping-off place for the Bay of Biscay. They collected special explosive, signal rockets, German ensigns, and much other vital material.

H.M.S. *Campbeltown* turned up on March 10. The Motor Launches, meanwhile, had gone to Southampton, Poole, and Appledore to have upper deck petrol tanks fitted for the long distance to be sailed. They also got two Oerlikon 20-mm. guns mounted on each vessel. The original estimate of eight to twelve M.L.s carrying only about a couple of hundred men soon needed revision. It would be absolutely imperative to have some ships capable of dealing with chance encounters on the way. A Motor Gun Boat (314) and a Motor Torpedo Boat came to the rescue, and four more M.L.s carrying torpedoes were added to the dozen so far included.

The one snag was that the Motor Gun Boat, which had been earmarked to spearhead the attack, did not have enough fuel tanks for the trip, but Ryder was adamant on having the M.G.B. because she had radar and an echo-sounder installed—the only vessel to be so equipped. No additional tanks could be made available, so they were obtained somehow direct from the manufacturers—strictly against all regulations! With these extra tanks, and by towing her throughout the voyage to St Nazaire, it became possible to include the M.G.B., which in fact was to form the headquarters ship which Ryder and Newman used. Only by such unconventional and improvized means was the little flotilla ever eventually ready to set sail.

One more boat—and one more difficulty—had to be considered. Her name was just a number: M.T.B. 74. Her virtue, that she could torpedo the dock gate if the *Campbeltown* failed for any reason. The difficulty was that she could not do any speeds of *more* than six knots or *less* than thirty-three! As the average of the convoy was to be about twelve knots, she had to proceed in long hops followed by long rests! A 'wavy navy' sub-lieutenant commanded her, and it was good to note the predominance of these 'hostilities only' officers commanding the M.L.s and No. 74. The galaxy of V.C.s subsequently awarded reflected greatly on them—as the regular Royal Navy officers who won the cross readily acknowledged. Two Hunt-class destroyers were detailed as escorts.

Although at first it was assumed that *Campbeltown* would be the headquarters ship, Colonel Newman said he favoured a smaller vessel, in case the destroyer should get stuck on one of the many mud-flats which were one of the hazards of the Loire Estuary. There could be nothing worse than to try to conduct an operation from a ship stuck helplessly away from the scene of the landings. Newman and Commander Ryder decided therefore to make the Motor Gun Boat their H.Q. for the actual attack, transferring to her from *Campbeltown* before arrival.

The scheme began to take shape. They would lead the force up river in M.G.B. 314, followed on each flank by M.L.s 160 and 270 with their torpedoes ready to deal with any enemy naval force. Then would come *Campbeltown* and

fourteen more M.L.s with the fast-and-slow M.T.B. 74
astern.

Just as more boats had been called for, so the military
force, or Commandos, was realized to be inadequate. It
was increased from 150 to 277. The naval personnel numbered 353, making 630 for the assault. The Commandos
were to land at three pre-selected points. One group would
go ashore north of the Old Mole; a second on both sides of
the Old Entrance to the harbour; and the third scramble
from *Campbeltown* while she was jammed in the dock gate
and deal with the various installations near the lock which
were mentioned earlier.

After all the demolition work had been done, the three
groups were to re-assemble near the Old Mole promontory
for embarkation and escape back to Britain. It was a
daring plan, and although in the ensuing few weeks the
commanders made it as foolproof as possible, much could
—and did—go wrong. So many things just could not
possibly be foreseen.

To approach even fairly near undetected seemed to be
one of the hardest problems. First, the nineteen vessels
would have to avoid being picked up by the radar station
in Cap Le Croisie. Second, the noise of so many boats all
steaming along together might be heard too soon. To
lessen the chances of either of these fears being realized,
an air plan was devised to divert the attention of the coastal
defences and generally to upset them. Seventy Welling-
tons would distract the radar station and swamp the sound
of the attacking ships. The air attack was due to begin
forty minutes before the zero hour of landings and continue right up to the minute the men stepped ashore. The
target area was the docks.

As is usual with such operations, the combination of
suitable weather and tide restricted the date and time. It
had to take place on a moonlit night with a high tide be-

tween midnight and 2 A.M., so that *Campbeltown* could cross the mud-flats as safely as possible. The destroyer's draught was reduced to some 10½ feet and the shallowest parts were 14 feet—only a yard to spare! All the vessels had to be clear of the area by daybreak, moreover, which meant a departure time of 4 A.M. at the latest after the raid.

The only dates possible proved to be five days commencing on the night of March 29–30.

The forces and approximate date settled, preparations pushed ahead with all possible priority. The craft had to be altered in several ways to fit them for a round trip up to 1000 miles—far more than the range in the mind of their designers. The M.L.s got their two Oerlikons each and extra petrol tanks. These M.L.s had little protection against bullets other than light plating round their bridge. Furthermore, being wooden, they represented a serious fire risk with the extra fuel on deck. The twenty-eight Oerlikons on the fourteen M.L.s, however, were thought to possess distinct advantages against shore batteries or air strafing on the return journey. Later on, in the actual action, their rapid-firing and brilliant tracer was to shatter the night by sound and sight.

As well as reducing the draught of the *Campbeltown*, the other alteration to the centrepiece ship of the operation was the arrangement of the explosive charge.

To lessen the draught, some armament was removed, while the bridge became screened by bullet-proof plating with slits for steering and vision generally. The two after-funnels were removed, too, and the foremost funnels cut on a slope to give the ship a striking resemblance to German torpedo boats.

As for the explosive, the initial idea had been to ram the lock first, then carry all the explosive up towards the bows, fuse it, and fire it by a delay mechanism. This plan obviously had grave disadvantages: carting five tons along a dark deck badly buckled was not the least of them. But if the charge were built in beforehand the difficulty was to know how far back from the bows to place it. If it were too near, the mechanism for fusing it would be smashed by the impact of the ship against the lock; if it were too far back, it would eventually explode some yards away from the concrete of the lock and not penetrate and breach the dock. Yet another obstacle to be overcome was how to be sure that the ship could be scuttled satisfactorily.

Lieutenant N. Tibbets, D.S.C., R.N., appointed as demolition expert to Commander Ryder, finally proposed that the ship should be scuttled soon after ramming the dock. This did not mean that it would sink. Only the stern half from amidships should really settle in the water as the bows would be jammed high and dry against the gate. Several systems for fusing the five tons were evolved to meet every eventuality, and the plan fixed for the explosion to occur some hours after the raiders had left St Nazaire. And furthermore, at least one of the fuses worked under water. So nothing could go wrong.

The charge was accommodated in twenty-four depth-charge cases placed in a special tank. The charges were all laced together with 'cord-text,' an instantaneous water-proof fuse, which would ensure simultaneous detonation. Yet even if the charge did not detonate for some unforeseen reason, the ship would still have sunk and be blocking the entrance to the dock—a comforting thought.

The alterations to the destroyer were begun on March 10 and completed within ten days, leaving Lieutenant Commander Beattie some valuable time to become used to handling her and get in some practice with her new guns. Despite all efforts to reduce draught, she still required some 12 feet when travelling at speeds over 15 knots. So she could count on clearing the mud by only a matter of inches—perhaps not at all.

Devonport had distinct advantages as a base and departure port, but Falmouth was finally considered more suitable. It was nearer; and every mile counted in an operation which would stretch fuel and resources to their fullest. Against Falmouth could be reckoned the belief that a spy operated there. To account for the presence of even so modest a force as nineteen vessels, a 'cover-plan' had to be conceived which overcame all questions of security. So the story went out that the force was forming up at Falmouth to train as a long-range anti-submarine striking group to be used to intercept U-boats returning to their bases in the Bay of Biscay—one of which, incidentally, was St Nazaire itself, so the tale had an element of truth in it!

An exercise off Plymouth the week before the attack revealed that massed searchlights from the shore aimed at a low angle to spot approaching ships could dazzle beyond belief and make navigation very awkward. The exercise also demonstrated that all the craft would be better painted in a dark colour, as the usual light greys of camouflage showed up badly under searchlight.

The two escort destroyers, *Atherstone* and *Tynedale*, slipped into Falmouth on March 23, and berthed well away from the M.L.s already assembled there. The Commandos had been kept on board for some days to learn their complicated manœuvres. With the arrival of *Campbeltown* on the 25th all was at last ready.

As the weather had been fine for five days, with a light easterly wind—just what was wanted—Newman and Ryder decided that the sooner they got away the better. The sail to St Nazaire would take a day and a half by the devious Atlantic route chosen for safety, so they fixed the attack for the night of 27th–28th, and made a rendezvous off Falmouth at 1427, just before half past two, on the afternoon of March 26. The waiting was over.

With the last light of that day, an escorting Hurricane

made a final orbit round the assorted convoy below and veered northward for the Lizard and home.

The last link with England gone, the ships steamed south-west into the night. Almost due south of Land's End they turned more towards the French coast and continued right through the night, passing a hundred miles or more clear of Brest and the north-west tip of France about midnight. By 0400, before daybreak, they were still sailing more or less due south many miles out into the Atlantic and drew level with Lorient, a famous U-boat base.

The day dawned with maximum visibility and a cloudless sky, too bright for their purpose. There was still nothing to report. Ryder came up to the bridge of *Campbeltown* about 0700 to see Beattie.

The next twenty-four hours would be decisive. In eighteen hours they would have gone into St Nazaire, and in a further six have got away again. On this blue-grey-silver morning in March it all seemed rather unreal. St Nazaire lay nearly a couple of hundred miles due east now; there was nothing in sight but sea—and the little ships.

Suddenly at 0705 escort destroyer *Tynedale* made a signal:

"Suspicious object on horizon to north."

Ryder was now aboard the *Atherstone*.

"What did you see?" he signalled.

"May be submarine or fishing boat, now bearing 002."

Atherstone again:

"Close and investigate. Will follow you when tow is slipped."

Then to *Campbeltown*:

"Take charge in my absence. S/M has been sighted."

Meanwhile *Tynedale* tore into the attack. It was imperative that no message should get back to the U-boat's base of a convoy heading for St Nazaire.

As she swung round to the attack her bows cut deep

furrows of wake in the water—as if she were actually ploughing a course through the foam. She put on more speed and dropped depth charges. A few second's silence, then the deep shattering cracks from the Bay of Biscay. The Captain scanned the sea with his glasses, but no sign of wreckage.

Signal from Ryder in M.G.B. to *Tynedale*:

"Did you see conning-tower before you depth-charged?'

"Yes, but no marking. S/M was trying to surface."

Then she must have thought better of it and dived quickly!

Further signal from *Tynedale*:

"Sub. had little time to make report. Consider she is damaged."

The evidence for this was that *Tynedale* had got to within two and a half miles of the U-boat and fired a shallow depth-charge pattern causing her to break surface astern. *Tynedale* shot up the sub., which subsided.

Ryder summed up the situation to *Tynedale*:

"Consider that a sighting report may have been made. Unless this is followed up by reconnaissance aircraft and further sighting, intend to continue operation."

From *Tynedale*:

"Your 0939. Consider it unlikely that S/M sighted M.L.s. Possible enemy appreciation will be that we are two destroyers on passage to Gibraltar."

"Agree."

The two escorts then rejoined the force, and *Atherstone* took M.G.B. 314 in tow again. No peace now, though.

A whole host of fishing trawlers loomed into view. The raiders had altered course eastward after the U-boat incident, so were now gradually getting nearer to the coast. The last thing they wanted was to be recognized and reported by trawlers which might well have been sympathetic to the Vichy collaborationist government in France, so a pre-arranged plan was put into operation. M.G.B. 314 went over to one of them, *Le Slack*, and Lieutenant Curtis, who spoke French, led a boarding party. There was no opposition; just the opposite. The crew helped them as much as they could with chart and other information, and so it was decided to chance the trawlers and let them go. It would have been too much of an undertaking to sink them all, anyway, and accommodate their crews.

Things began to take a turn for the better. Friendly fishermen, and now low clouds came across the sky. In case of over-optimism, however, a signal from C-in-C, Plymouth, brought them back to realities. It told them that five enemy torpedo-boats had been reported off St Nazaire. As these were superior to the M.L.s, another couple of Hunt-class destroyers, *Cleveland* and *Brocklesby*, were to be sailed from Falmouth to help the raiders when they withdrew next day.

Anything could happen, still. The nineteen ships sailed in a special formation to maintain the deception, if spotted from the air, that they were an anti-submarine sweep. To conceal further their real intention of attacking St Nazaire, they steered slightly south of due east, apparently heading considerably further down the French coast. This was a vital stage. They had to survive till darkness without being discovered. The afternoon dragged past. Suspense and suppressed excitement filled every one.

At 2005 they stopped; the headquarters was transferred from *Atherstone* to M.G.B. 314; they formed into fighting order with the M.G.B. out in front; and they swung up to a north-easterly course—straight for the Loire and St Nazaire. Five hours more and they would reach their goal. Still the essential element was surprise—for as long as possible.

They set sail. M.L. 341 reported engine trouble, so transferred her men to one of the three spare M.L.s astern.

The force headed for position Z. Ten o'clock at night, forty miles off an enemy port, and a secret rendezvous at a position Z. An exciting prospect. The meeting was still more thrilling—with a British submarine, *Sturgeon*, which was waiting submerged until the approach of the convoy and then surfaced to show a screened light to seaward as beacon.

At this point the escort destroyers broke away leaving the strange force to complete the last lap alone. The lights of a large number of fishing vessels away to port northward indicated that the raiders were still undetected. Detection by radar would also prove more difficult with so many ships in the vicinity.

The Commandos and sailors began to hold their breath almost by now, as they glided through the water on a still, silent night.

By midnight they were seventeen or so miles out. Gun-flashes began to be seen in the distance to the north-east. At 0030 they were ten miles offshore, and it became clear that heavy air activity was in progress. Gun-flashes and flak burst over a wide area. But the air attack was not going according to plan. With an overcast sky and light drizzle, the bombers could not see their targets. As attacks were not allowed unless the targets could be distinctly identified, owing to the risk of killing civilians, most of the bombers brought their loads back again—a devastating blow to the overall assault. The planes had alerted all the defences in the area without causing the chaos for which they had been specifically included in the attack. Whether or not the results would prove serious remained to be seen. Fortunately as the ships sailed in they were oblivious to this alarming development.

At 0045 land was sighted, five miles off. M.G.B. 314 echo-sounded the bottom for shoals. They were crossing the mud-flats now. The time was 0100. Beattie on the bridge of the *Campbeltown* kept her to 10 knots for quiet. Suddenly the speed slackened to 7–8 knots. She had touched the bottom, but without increasing engine revolutions she shoved clear. Again the same thing happened, and again she got off and caught up the few lost yards.

Into the mouth of the estuary they went; their excitement turning to cheerfulness. They were nearer the northern shore now: less than two miles out, and running parallel to it. A mile and a half away it was.

A mile and a half out, the bright beam of a searchlight swept astern of the ships. Then it went off. Both banks had hidden danger—coastal defences or anti-aircraft batteries. Beattie's eyes narrowed as he peered through the slits in the protective plating of *Campbeltown*. Ryder and Newman crouched under cover in M.G.B. 314—the first in the line: a dangerous place to be.

So far so good. No minefields or obstructions had been met; nor had there been any casualties on the mud-flats. At 0122, when they were a mile and a quarter out, searchlights suddenly skimmed the water from both banks, blazing beams of light which blinded Beattie as he took *Campbeltown* towards her position for the final ramming. Every craft must have been silhouetted in this intense concentration, but they were painted dark and flew tattered ensigns, and *Campbeltown* looked like a German torpedo-boat.

They sailed in. They were challenged from shore: a coast battery first, then one from the dockyard. A minute had passed, but each second was precious if they were to reach their objective.

0123. It was for this very moment that Leading Signalman Pike had been attached to Ryder. He could send and receive German morse, so made a succession of K's which was the sign of a friendly ship. This delayed the onslaught from the shore. Then he launched into a long message about having been "damaged by enemy action" and "requested permission to proceed up harbour without delay." An amazing deception only a mile from shore. The challenging firing stopped for a second.

Fire from the north bank broke out: still restrained fire, as if the Germans were not sure what to think or do. M.G.B. 314 made the "friendly forces" signal with its brightest Aldis lamp, and the firing ceased!

In six more minutes *Campbeltown* would be home. Already she was past most of the heavy batteries.

Three of those minutes passed; then at 0127 the force was fired on in earnest from all sides. There was no point now in not replying. The *Campbeltown* opened up first, followed by all the others.

Fire screamed in a four-way exchange—from both shores to ships, and ships to both shores. Almost horizontal tracer tore across the harbour only a few feet above water level. M.G.B. 314 came up to the flak ship on guard duty. The ship lay less than half a mile from the dock gate. At two hundred yards from her, the M.G.B. saw the vessel floodlit in the full glare of a searchlight—and three bursts of pom-pom fire silenced her in a second.

"Well done, Savage," called Ryder to the Able Seaman gun-layer lying in an exposed position near the bows of the M.G.B. The poor flak ship got hits from each of the convoy on passing, and also intercepted fire from its own shore guns aiming at the British ships. Finally she scuttled herself to escape the holocaust.

The gun-layers of all the coastal craft were doing a wonderful job, for after a further three minutes the shore fire slackened considerably. The momentary respite enabled Beattie to swing *Campbeltown* round and head her for the lock. She was hard to handle, with a large turning circle, and still he was being blinded partially by searchlights. The responsibility for running in on course was great. There would be no second chance. Once ashore, the ship could not be 'backed' for another try at the target.

Yet still the firing came. Beattie stepped up the speed to twenty knots. The coxswain was shot away from the wheel. Beattie controlled her from the after-wheelhouse. She raced past the Old Mole promontory on her port side, only 200 yards off.

Now a quarter of a mile remained between her and the dock. She completed her change of course port. Beattie checked direction. There was less than a minute to go. Thirty seconds, two hundred yards. She felt a slight drag as she cut the torpedo net.

At 0134, four minutes after the intended time, she struck the lock caisson squarely, with a crash. The M.L.s heard the impact clearly, but Beattie did not feel it as strongly as he had expected. The engine room men did not even know they had rammed.

Beattie went down below to see that the troops were getting ashore satisfactorily, then he looked out and saw the fo'csle deck high and dry over the top of the lock gate. Down below the water-line of the ship, the bows had buckled back to a distance of some 35 feet—exactly the amount calculated and wanted.

Eighty or so Commandos scrambled ashore over the fo'csle, down their scaling ladders, and on to their tasks. The eight Oerlikons of the destroyer kept up a covering fire during this landing, which was being bitterly opposed. Scuttling charges were fused and the explosive charge near the bows, which was now right up against the lock, a perfect position to wreck it when the charge went off, finally fixed. The ship began to sink slowly, settling by the stern. She had suffered badly and an M.L. came alongside to take off the injured.

In the hail of fire during those few mad minutes of the approach into the harbour, much of the plan so meticu-

lously worked out on paper had to be drastically revised
—even abandoned. As the *Campbeltown* sped towards the
lock gates, the M.L.s were in twin columns astern, one
port and one starboard. The port column were to land
their Commandos near the Old Mole, it will be remembered, and the starboard column continue on and swing
in nearer the harbour, on each side of its Old Entrance.

Under the bombardment, M.L. 192 leading the starboard six was hit early. She was carrying the senior officer
of the M.L.s and troops detailed for the Old Entrance
assault. She caught fire, crossed to the port column, and
turned in to beach herself in the shallow water south of the
Old Mole. M.L.s 262 and 267 following missed their
landing-place in the great glare and proceeded too far
up-river. M.L. 268, fourth in the column, turned in correctly but was hit while approaching the Old Entrance and
enveloped in flames. M.L. 156 came next, but she had been
hit hard very early in the action. Her steering-gear shattered and most of her military and naval personnel injured
or killed, she turned out of line somehow and withdrew
on one remaining engine.

Last in the line to starboard came M.L. 177, undeterred
and undaunted. She swung round successfully into the Old
Entrance and landed her troops on the south side. Leader
of the whole nineteen ships, M.G.B. 314, who had been
giving valuable covering fire for *Campbeltown*, followed the
M.L. in, and Colonel Newman and his staff were landed.
Ryder told M.L. 177 by land-hailer to hurry to *Campbeltown* and take off survivors, as already mentioned.

M.G.B. 314, the headquarters ship still, then turned and
lay up against the steps of the north side of the Old
Entrance—bows pointing out.

The two M.L.s who had missed their mark turned and
landed their troops, but these parties were repulsed
severely and forced to re-embark almost at once. Cascades

of fire forced the M.L.s to cast off—back to the fire and fury of the harbour. Thus the only M.L. of the starboard column to get its Commandos ashore according to plan was No. 177.

The Old Entrance adjoined the lock-gate end of the dock where the *Campbeltown* lay, so it can be seen that the destroyer and her crew were uncomfortably close to the strong enemy guns around the Old Entrance.

As *Campbeltown* rammed the lock and the six starboard M.L.s struggled against superior gunfire further up-harbour, the column of seven M.L.s to port turned sharply in to the Old Mole, situated on the Ile de St Nazaire. The Commandos aboard knew that their task was to capture the island, isolate it by demolishing bridges and lock gates connecting it to the mainland, and hold the Old Mole as the point to re-embark all the forces landed.

Fire and flames flashed across the waters as before.

M.L. 447 led the column round, was hit by flak, and burst into flames. M.L. 457 got her troops through the barrage defending the Old Mole, but circling round afterwards was attacked and hit while backing into the slightly calmer waters midstream. M.L. 307 passed 447 on fire, closed into the Old Mole, was struck by flak and grenades, and suffered heavy casualties. They could not get in, so withdrew and engaged batteries and searchlights on the opposite bank of the river.

M.L. 443 overshot the mark in the midst of searing searchlights, returned to the Old Mole, but could not land her troops. M.L. 306 found M.L. 192 burning to the south and No. 447 to the north, so circled round under heavy fire in an attempt to get alongside. She could not—so withdrew. M.L. 446 did the same. Series of splitting shells and bullets wounded most of the troops, including the officers and sergeant. The only course was to withdraw.

As at the Old Entrance, only one M.L.—No. 457 this

time—got through the overwhelming defences. That
accounted for most of the M.L.s, but the pair right in the
spearhead of the assault, just behind the M.G.B., had
been placed there to torpedo or shoot up any craft challenging the raiders' approach. They met none, so proceeded to their next task—providing covering fire for
Campbeltown as she went into the attack. M.L. 270 was hit
in her stern off the Old Entrance and had to withdraw,
resorting to hand steering. M.L. 160 on the port side, the
St Nazaire bank of the estuary, bombarded a specific flak
emplacement north of the landing positions, then fired her
torpedoes at an enemy vessel by the south jetties.

Looking round for ways in which he could help other
craft in distress, the commanding officer of M.L. 160 saw
No. 447 still ablaze, went alongside with the flames fanned
across the gap in a threatening manner, and rescued most
of the personnel on board. And all the while, M.L. 160
came under devastating point-blank fire from pill-boxes
on the Old Mole.

Last of the M.L.s was No. 298, which passed through
petrol burning on the water; caught fire, becoming a mark
for enemy gunners; and eventually blew up.

Aboard Motor Gun Boat 314 Ryder watched the crazy
geometric patterns made by the 'perforations' of tracer
as it sped low through the night sky. A burst early on had
broken the wireless aerial, so the boat became isolated
from other W/T contact among the raiders.

Ryder directed the M.G.B. to be berthed on the north
—Normandie Dock—side of the Old Entrance. Already
many of the ship's company of the *Campbeltown* had been
taken off by M.L. 177. The rest came running down the
steps towards the M.G.B., some of them seriously wounded.
Ryder checked that *Campbeltown* was completely evacu-
ated. Guarded by Leading Signalman Pike, he dashed
over to the destroyer. Four scuttling charges exploded as

they watched her, sending them hurrying back again. The M.G.B. was coming under very heavy fire now, but Ryder kept the M.G.B. on this exposed point between the Old Entrance and the Dock until all the wounded were aboard. Looking over his shoulder as they returned to the M.G.B. he saw the *Campbeltown*'s stern already awash.

Meanwhile, above all the roar, the sound of demolition coming from the pumping-house regions reassured them all that the Commandos from the *Campbeltown* were well away on their disruptive duties.

M.G.B. 314 moved on from the lock to the Old Mole to see what the situation looked like there. Before leaving, Ryder told M.T.B. 74 to shoot her torpedoes at the Old Entrance. The tubes hit the lock gates of the Entrance. Then she hastened back to the Gunboat, took off nine survivors from the crowded decks (which were living targets) and set course for home at 40 knots.

It was half past two in the morning when the M.G.B. came round towards the Old Mole, and Ryder could see that this 'embarkation point' was still stoutly defended by the enemy. The dark waters of the Loire leaped alight with spilt petrol bursting into flames—an amazing middle-of-the-night scene. The pill-box on the mole still spat out fire: the M.G.B. engaged it. Able Seaman Savage—the pom-pom gun-layer—sent a burst towards the pill-box, then a second which entered the embrasure and silenced it.

Savage then took on skyline gun positions on surrounding buildings, but a Bofors battery on the opposite bank began to get the range of the gunboat. Then the pill-box leaped to life again.

The gunboat was thus being attacked from three sides—each flank of the Old Entrance and from the Bofors—and was fighting for her life. Savage silenced the pill-box a second time, but the boat was being hit almost continuously. By a miracle only it still floated. The sole gun

remaining in action was the pom-pom, to which Savage
stuck throughout this three-sided battle. The Bofors received a direct hit, and Savage was killed—heroically.

Ryder told Curtis, in charge of the M.G.B., to go into
the entrance again, but the fight grew fiercer and they
could not tell friend from foe. Some one had boarded
Campbeltown and fired one of the Oerlikons across the Old
Entrance.

The position was becoming desperate. The maximum
time for the operation had been fixed for two hours, and
already one hour and sixteen minutes had passed. Both
possible places of embarkation were in enemy hands.
Looking round the river, Ryder saw no other craft—only
eight blazing wrecks, sunk or on fire. The M.G.B. had
forty or more survivors, many critically injured. A decision
had to be taken urgently. They dropped a smoke float,
had a hurried conference in the midst of the action, and
decided that the time had come to go. Miraculous as it
seemed, neither the steering-gear nor the engines had been
damaged. Curtis gave the order "full speed downstream"
and the boat moved out at 24 knots.

The Commandos' attack does not really come within
the scope of the naval V.C. story—but it must be put on
record that they achieved most of their objects despite
the small numbers which could be landed. Colonel Newman was taken prisoner, but, before this, had inspired his
men to breath-taking exploits in the docks and even in the
main street of St Nazaire.

The position was a difficult one. The main objective—
ramming the dock gate—had been accomplished, but
whether the explosive would detonate correctly remained
to be seen. Some of the subsidiary targets had been dealt
with, others, not. Casualties had been heavier than hoped.

Still the withdrawal of the rest had to be effected.
M.G.B. 314 moved over to the south bank of the river, and

kept up her 24 knots. Searchlights soon spotted her flight, but luckily the smoke floats she was dropping engaged their attention more than the gunboat itself. The shore batteries were firing astern of her, hitting the smoke!

She overtook a limping M.L. and made smoke with the chloro-sulphonic acid equipment in the hope of protecting the craft. The flak began to fade a little, when suddenly a salvo from a heavy coast battery fell a few yards ahead of the boat, spraying her as she ploughed out of the estuary.

By now, Newman had won his V.C.; Savage, a second one; Ryder, a third; and Beattie of the *Campbeltown*, a fourth.

Beattie and other officers of the *Campbeltown* had been taken on M.L. 177, which set off downstream at a brisk 15 knots, making her leaving signal about 0220. The chances for her escape seemed good. Then after ten minutes, two hits set her afire. She drifted down-river blazing. The crew and *Campbeltown* officers clambered overboard. Beattie got an arm over the side of a raft, clung on—and dozed off to sleep! For four hours M.L. 177 burned. For longer than this the survivors held on to hope and life.

Meanwhile the searchlights had lost M.G.B. 314, who had altered course southward. The gunfire was radar controlled, however, and not until four miles offshore did they give up the fight. Ryder and the rest watched the flash of guns along the coast heralding heavy salvos landing in the water around them several seconds later.

Ahead, they seemed to be gaining ground—or water—on another M.L. They closed towards her and found out too late it was an enemy patrol vessel. She opened fire on the M.G.B. at short range. A stream of tracer ripped into one of the petrol tanks. They waited for the boat to burst into flames, but it did not. The only gun still working was the pom-pom, but as the M.G.B. swerved away this could not be brought to bear on the enemy. Further afield, she swung back again, and a few accurate shots with the pom-pom stopped the enemy's firing and started a fire.

Next on the scene was M.L. 270, steering by hand. The M.G.B. cut her speed to 12 knots and stayed with the M.L. As an added hazard, the sea seemed to be exceptionally phosphorescent that night, so that the bow waves and the wakes were lit up as brightly as in daylight.

By 0430 the M.G.B. reached the rendezvous point Y but did not stop, in view of the radically altered plans of the entire little fleet. About two hours later, the gunboat and M.L. 270 observed heavy action to eastward, which later proved to be the destroyer *Tynedale* in a running action with five German torpedo-boats. Both *Tynedale* and *Atherstone* altered course south to lead the enemy away from the smaller craft. In the fight that followed *Tynedale* came under the five vessel's concentrated fire for nine minutes and was hit twice. She saw hits on the third enemy ship. Then she made smoke and broke off the action at 0645.

The M.G.B. and M.L. 270 were cheered to see M.L. 156 coming up astern and M.L. 446 a mile away to the north. In addition to these four, a further four had managed to get away from the Loire: M.L.s 443, 307, 160 and 306.

Others had been less lucky. M.L. 267 was abandoned on fire in the night. M.L. 298 got only one mile before being set on fire. M.T.B. 74, the 40-knot craft, which could have been well on her way home, had gallantly gone to the rescue of one of the burning M.L.s and was set on fire herself.

Now in the early dawning, *Atherstone* stopped and took off the crew of M.L. 156. Then the escort destroyer came on to the M.G.B. After its heroic hours, the shabby gunboat presented a picture both poignant and proud. As the commander of the *Atherstone* surveyed the scene he saw the little boat holed in many places, particularly forward, and he bit his lip as his eyes looked down on many, many men wounded and suffering on the deck—which was slippery with their blood. The sea was flat, yet even so, getting the wounded aboard *Atherstone* proved no easy affair.

While *Atherstone* took on the crew of M.L. 156 and the wounded of the gallant gunboat, *Tynedale* was embarking the injured men from M.L.s 270 and 446. The vessels had to stop for a full half an hour, from 0720 to 0750, a sitting target. A Heinkel 115 actually appeared on the scene, circled the collection of ships, and then bombed and sank an abandoned M.L. astern!

By 0800 the force had formed up and was making 14 knots westward and away from the St Nazaire nightmare.

A Beaufighter greeted them: then a Junkers 88. The German was at once attacked by the Beaufighter. As if sensing the ordeal of the forces at sea level, and determined to protect them from further suffering, the pilot of the Beaufighter rammed the enemy plane in mid-air over the vessels and was killed.

Back in the estuary of the Loire, the sun had come up and those of the M.L. 177 who had not been drowned were picked up by a German trawler and made prisoners of war, among them Lieutenant-Commander Beattie. The rest of the war, three years and more, he spent in a prison camp in Germany.

Besides the H.Q. force, M.L.s 160, 307, and 443 also failed to make contact at the rendezvous point. So they made up for a pre-arranged position 46° N and 7° W, thence to sail up the meridian. On their way, however, enemy bombers struck them several times. A Heinkel III was the first unwise enough to try to sink the intrepid trio, but their concentrated fire sent it crashing into the sea. Next a large Blomm and Voss seaplane withdrew diffidently after being hit. Detouring many miles out into the

Atlantic to avoid further unwelcome visitors, these three eventually reached Falmouth quite alone, and with no more than a gallon or two of petrol between them.

M.L. 341, whose engine had broken down before the attack, also reached a home port after a long voyage without any escort—another amazing achievement in waters infested with U-boats and enemy patrol vessels. All her troops had been transferred to another M.L. as soon as her engine trouble was first noticed.

The operation was still far from finished, however. Not until the morning of the 28th, about nine o'clock, did Ryder hear of the end of M.L. 306. Her memory may be dimmed, but the last minutes deserve to go down in the annals of valour; for it was to recognize such spirit as this that the three V.C.s were awarded to the St Nazaire navy men.

M.L. 306 had made repeated attempts to land her troops at the Old Mole, according to orders; but at 0200, with only one Oerlikon still serviceable, she left St Nazaire, speeding at 18 knots and making smoke as she sailed. She succeeded in getting clear of the coast. Just before first flush of light, though, she sighted five large ships on the port bow coming close past. The Captain did not know if they were friend or foe, so stopped engines hoping to pass unobserved. It was still dark and the ships passed only 100 yards off without seeing her.

When they were clear, the captain started up engines— whereupon a single searchlight swung round from the last ship of the line. The unidentified craft were the five enemy torpedo-boats. They circled the poor lone M.L. considering the kill. They opened fire with small arms. The boat's one Oerlikon and two Bren guns manned by the Commandos responded valiantly. Then the enemy decided to ram. But the M.L. swung sharply round, escaping with a glancing blow, yet enough to fling several men into the

water. As the enemy ship drew away she raked the M.L.
with short-range weapons. At 50 yards she crashed 4-inch
shells into the British boat. The bridge was hit; the captain,
Lieutenant I. B. Henderson, R.N.V.R., was killed, and the
rest of the officers were wounded. The enemy closed to
come alongside and hailed the M.L. in broken English.
Nearly everyone aboard was injured, so the little ship had
to surrender. The men were taken prisoner.

All this Ryder learned later.

As soon as C.-in-C., Plymouth, heard of the five torpedo-
boats in the Bay, the two escort destroyers were doubled
in number by the despatch to the scene of a further pair,
Cleveland and *Brocklesby*. They joined the remnants of the
raiders at 0906.

The situation still seemed dangerous and difficult, for
since the loss of the Beaufighter, the enemy had the air to
themselves, and the cloudy sky looked just right for bombing attacks.

A breeze blew up from the north-west, and the damaged
M.L.s became slower and slower, and began to ship water.
This was tantalizing, for the destroyers wanted to sail at
full speed with the wounded, many of whom might not live
unless treated promptly.

A couple of air attacks on the craft—now reduced to
10 knots—were repulsed without damage, and *Brocklesby*
shot down a Junkers 88, which spiralled into the sea. The
speed continued intolerably slow. Commander G. B.
Sayer, R.N., of the *Cleveland*, had taken over charge of the
journey home, allowing Ryder and the others to sleep. He
made a careful survey of the situation and decided to
transfer all personnel to the destroyers and scuttle the three
limping M.L.s. By 1350 this was done, enabling the four
fast destroyers to step-up their speed to 25 knots.

Back at St Nazaire the morning moved on. At daybreak
a strong cordon of German troops were thrown around

both sides of the lock. About the same time that Beattie was being picked out of the sea, an inspection party of forty or more German officers threaded their way over the approaches to the lock gate and clambered up on board *Campbeltown*, to see how she could best be moved. The destroyer had settled by the stern now, of course. Her bows were still wedged over the top of the gate. With the inspection party walked the German Admiral in charge of the whole port.

French dock workers were barred from the lock, but the assembly had been swollen by German soldier sightseers. The officers poked about here and there near the bows, uttering guttural oaths about the awkward predicament.

The Admiral returned the salute of port naval officers and stepped ashore. His chauffeur opened the car door, and he vanished back to his offices. The officers continued their tour of exploration. Soldiers huddled round the lock gate.

Far out in the Bay of Biscay, Sayer had just decided to scuttle the M.L.s.

Suddenly a thunderous explosion shook the city. Every window in St Nazaire within a mile of the dock shattered, splintered. The *Campbeltown* had gone up. The lock gate was smashed. Sixty enemy officers and 320 men lay dead or dying.

The twenty-four depth charges, each of 200 lb., were within a yard or so of the caisson. Five tons of high explosive had done its worst. As the smoke cleared, the forward half of the ship was seen to have disintegrated—as far aft as the foremost funnel. The water surged into the dock; the after half of *Campbeltown* was swept down the dock; two merchantmen surged forward, too, with thousands of gallons of water. A chaotic cauldron bubbling, foaming, frothing, roaring, rushing.

The main mission was accomplished.

The British destroyers drew level with Brest by evening. At 1850, *Cleveland* contacted the other three M.L.s, 160, 443, and 307, and she took *Brocklesby* out as far as the 7° W meridian to try to find them. Meanwhile, *Atherstone* and *Tynedale* put on all possible speed with the wounded and made Plymouth in the very early hours of the following morning. By a coincidence, they docked at 0145 on March 29—exactly twenty-four hours after the attack, when the battle was at its height.

"A lot can happen in a day," Ryder observed to Sayer.

At last Ryder had time to think, to compare the blueprint for the raid with the event itself. He realized what a tragedy it was that Bomber Command could drop scarcely a single bomb because of bad weather. As things turned out, all the air raid really accomplished was to raise the alarm. Guns were already manned; duty and fire patrols had fallen in or were standing by; the look-out system had been alerted. All that the gun crews had to do when they finally realized that an enemy force was sailing up the estuary was lower their weapons, all of which were dual-purpose and sited to defend the waterfront. Wooden M.L.s could hardly have been easier targets.

As Ryder received reports from the individual commanders of craft he gradually began to see the whole operation in a clearer perspective. He appreciated more, too, the way in which the navigator for the force, Lieutenant A. R. Green, R.N., had piloted the force unerringly up the Loire Estuary without the aid of lights or buoys. This he did after a voyage of 450 miles—and yet *Campbeltown* hit the dock only four minutes after calculated time!

Still the story remains unfinished. Not for several days were the full effects to be observed. Meanwhile, the German radio lost no time at all in representing the raid as a defeat for the Allies, even the repulse of a "second front" in Europe. They took advantage of the British delay in announcing the results to produce for inspection by neutral nations photographs they had taken of *Campbeltown* during the morning following the raid, but *before* she had exploded with such shattering effect.

As Ryder and Admiralty awaited reconnaissance photos—which were obtained ultimately on April 1—the rest of the story of St Nazaire was being written. About half-past four in the afternoon of the raid, just as the city was beginning to recover from the impact of the destroyer's explosion, one of M.T.B. 74's torpedoes blew up, its firing delay having run off. This shook the whole port area near the Old Entrance and blew one man into the Loire.

An hour later a second explosion shattered what was left of the Old Entrance. All the French workers anticipated trouble from the Germans and rushed towards the one remaining bridge to the town. But it was barred by enemy sentries. The Frenchmen overpowered them and rushed the bridge, but the sentries opened fire on them. Panic broke out all over the port. Most German officers were dead near the *Campbeltown*. The sentries turned their machine-guns on the throng of Frenchmen, killing many, for the Germans, of course, still imagined that Commandos were round every corner.

The air pictures duly arrived. They confirmed the complete success of *Campbeltown*'s first-time ramming. The outer caisson was destroyed. The inner caisson the Commandos had put out of action by hand-placed charges. The machinery for opening both outer and inner caissons was all destroyed, in one case the building housing it collapsing. The pumping machinery, also, could be written off, together with culverts and conduits deep down; heavy charges had been dropped into these. Indeed, so thorough did the destruction of the dock prove that four and a half years later it was still out of action—far beyond the end of the war.

Part of the secondary objectives failed. The attempt to obstruct the operation of U-boats by rendering the basins tidal was one example of these. Another was the neutralization of the concealed fuel depot adjacent to the Normandie Dock. But these were outweighed a pound to an ounce by the triumph of the *Campbeltown*.

Under the circumstances, cost of it all in terms of life and injury was not more than might have been expected.

Excluding the supporting forces the total naval and military men amounted to 630. Of these, 144 were killed: 23 per cent.

The analysis of the fate of the 630 is as follows:

Killed or missing	144
Prisoners of war	215
Returned to England	271
Total	630

Campbeltown had eighteen coastal craft with her in the attack. The enemy sunk ten; four were scuttled; and four reached England, including the immortal M.G.B. 314, from which Ryder and Newman had directed the operations, and in the bows of which Able Seaman Savage had died winning his Victoria Cross, awarded also "in recognition of the valour shown by many others in motor launches, the motor gunboat, and motor torpedo boat in this action."

13

FREDERICK THORNTON PETERS

A BIG, burly man was Captain Peters: a man for the attack, the right man, in fact, to be taking part in special Allied landings on the North African coast at Oran in November 1942. But his naval life started some thirty-seven years earlier—in 1905, when he was sixteen.

A brother officer has described him as "a typical Elizabethan gentleman adventurer. His entire soul was in the Navy. It was a fanaticism with him." He won the D.S.O. and D.S.C. during the 1914–18 war, beginning it with the rank of lieutenant, ending it as a commander. In 1919, when he was just thirty, he was one of the 400 young officers who had to be 'axed' when the personnel of the Navy was reduced.

Instead of moping, he accepted his lot and took a civilian job out on the Gold Coast—starting at the bottom as a clerk. Needless to say, he made good. Later on, he journeyed to Canada, where his father was an advocate in Montreal. As soon as war was declared, Peters worked his passage back to Britain in a tramp steamer, and within a month he was in the Navy commanding an anti-submarine flotilla on convoy work. In 1940 he won a bar to his D.S.C.

He was a lieutenant again now. Aboard the *Meteor* in an action on the Dogger Bank, the ship was hit. The commander shouted to ask where Peters was. The reply came:

"He's gone down to the boiler-room to turn off the steam-cocks."

The boiler-room is an uncomfortable place when a ship has been hit.

During 1942 Captain Peters was detailed for special service, which turned out to be to command an expedition in miniature to try to take Oran harbour. The two tiny ships comprising this 'fleet' were the ex-American coast-guard cutters *Walney* and *Hartland*.

Together these little cutters sped into the harbour at dead of night, crashed into the defences, and broke the boom. Peters stood on the bridge of the *Walney* and saw an enemy motor-launch ploughing straight for her. He swerved to avoid it, and was immediately caught in the concentrated beam of a Vichy-French searchlight. But they were through the boom, and that was one hazard over. The dash was still suicidal. The second *Walney* had been lit, every shore battery swivelled round on her and the searchlight kept her in constant view. As a barrage of fire flew over the water of the harbour, *Walney* was hit again and again. Peters did not let it deflect him one degree, but took her half-way up the harbour. The French guns were firing at closer range every second, and of the seventeen officers and men standing on the bridge of the cutter every one fell. Only Peters survived, though a bullet blinded him in one eye, and managed to steer the ship inshore, towards the quay which was the objective ordered.

The firing intensified as he approached. But he reached it.

He found a French cruiser lying there, which stopped *Walney's* shock troops, United States Rangers, from going ashore; so he ordered the cutter to be laid alongside the enemy. By now three submarines were on the attack, too, and *Walney* was ablaze. Somehow they shot grapnels into the deck of the cruiser. Boarding parties with tommy-guns at the ready stood by to carry the cruiser by storm. But the cutter had had enough. Her boilers burst, she leaned over exhausted, and sank.

Many of the men were drowned. Several, including Peters, got ashore on a Carley raft. Peters looked back from the raft as the ship went down, and the last part of her he saw was the flag flying to the end.

The other cutter, *Hartland*, had also reached the jetty by this time, but too few men remained alive for them to haul on the ropes and secure her. She drifted away again, blew up, and sank. So both small ships met the same fate.

Much later, the French picked up Peters and the others on the raft. He was taken before the French admiral in charge of the port and questioned closely. The Frenchman tried to make Peters admit having fired the first shot, which he would not do. So at length he was put in prison.

However, he spent only a short spell there, since Oran capitulated and the Free-French population broke in and bore Peters off literally shoulder-high through the streets, scattering flowers over him.

Peters was recommended for the American Distinguished Service Cross for this exploit carried out in company with the United States troops, but he never received this medal, for soon afterwards there came the sad announcement that a plane had crashed in North Africa. Among its occupants was Peters, already on another mission. Thus not one of the seventeen men on the bridge of the *Walney* that fateful night survived.

14

```
ROBERT ST VINCENT SHERBROOKE
```

WITH the turn of the year from 1942 to 1943 the tide had
really turned, too. The offensive spirit spread. After Oran
came the thrilling triumph of Captain Sherbrooke; and
how appropriate that the action on this particular run to
Russia should be marked by the V.C. For of all convoy
routes—indeed of all sea-lanes anywhere—during the war,
this was the worst. "The world's worst journey" it has
often been described as, and that is no exaggeration. Why
was it so bad? Because the combination of the enemy and
the elements, coupled with the imperative need for supplies to reach Russia from Britain all conspired to produce
conditions which made survival of ships—and men—hang
in the balance each time they set sail. The only course was
boldness. And it was just such brilliant bravado that
Sherbrooke showed.

He commanded the destroyer H.M.S. *Onslow* and served
as senior officer of all the destroyers escorting an important convoy headed for Russia. On New Year's Eve, the
convoy were off the North Cape, north of Norway: actually
on the morning of December 31.

All the ships were keeping their appointed station well,
but it was midwinter and heavy seas swelled around them.
Although the time approached noon, the day carried on
in an almost continual darkness, for they were not far from

the North Pole with its six-month, black-out. Conditions were all against mere men. The intense cold created navigational hazards in the form of ice freezing on to vital parts of the ships. What slight sight there was from daylight was curtailed by cloud, reducing surface visibility to a minimum, and even this semi-darkness was reduced further by frequent snowstorms.

In this setting, the convoy suddenly made contact with an enemy squadron of vastly superior strength. Usually in such situations little hope exists for the smaller ships. All other things equal, it is a case of cold statistics: the number and range of the larger ships' guns can hardly fail to outstrip their adversary. But all other things were not equal. The British convoy had in command Captain Sherbrooke.

The strength of the forces opposed to him was believed to be as follows: one pocket battleship, one cruiser, and a number of destroyers. It was the battleship and cruiser that counted.

Unhesitatingly, Sherbrooke aboard *Onslow* led his destroyers into the attack and closed with the enemy. The wild seas swirled to the bow-wake of destroyers of both sides, plus the two enemy capital ships, jockeying for positions to pierce the defence of the merchantmen—or from the British viewpoint, prevent it being pierced.

Four times the enemy vessels swung into the attack in the murky midday, to try to force a gap and get at the convoy. Four times they had to withdraw hurriedly behind a smokescreen. Even a screen was needed for their safety despite the gloom! The threat of torpedoes became too great for them.

Not content with just keeping them at bay behind their own smokescreen, Sherbrooke pursued them with *Onslow* and his small destroyer force. He worried them out of gunshot of the convoy, mauled them, intimidated them.

So the first of the four attacks was beaten off, and

brought home to the Germans' own ground—or sea. What was the precise power of the destroyers which were winning this scrap? The heaviest gun aboard *Onslow* had a calibre of 4·7-inch. Against this the *Lutzow* or *Admiral Scheer*, whichever pocket battleship it was, mounted no less than half a dozen 11-inch guns and eight 5·9-inch guns. And the cruiser, of similar tonnage to the battleship—about 10,000 —had at her command eight 8-inch guns. She turned out to be *Hipper*. Even the German destroyers mounted modern armament of five 5-inch guns. Thus the odds were overwhelming.

Into the second assault the enemy swept. By brilliant navigation, Sherbrooke once more headed them off. After the action had been in progress for forty minutes *Onslow* received a hit, as was almost inevitable. Then a second shell screamed into her, exploding with a roar above the wind and the water. The bridge was rocked and rent, and shrapnel splintered into a thousand particles. Several struck Sherbrooke, one right in the eye, depriving him of all sight for a second or two, but he gripped the remnant of the rail. He could see nothing from one eye. Agonized, he blinked the other eye open. Blood streamed from another wound, but he insisted on continuing to direct operations. For the second time the destroyers ran circles round the Germans, and not until he saw the smoke screen filtering through his remaining eye would he hear of receiving attention. Further hits on *Onslow* forced Sherbrooke to disengage and leave the enemy for the moment behind their hide-out. Even so, he refused the surgeon's plea to go below till he had made sure himself that the next senior officer had assumed control.

Sherbrooke staggered below, helped by the surgeon and a rating. The surgeon made him as comfortable as he could. The eye was worse, if anything.

"You must tell me how it's going," Sherbrooke whis-

pered and he meant it. The state of the battle was reported
to him for the next hour. Two more attacks were repulsed
in the second hour of the engagement. The credit for the
first half of the battle went largely to him and his cool,
prompt decisions. That the rest of it went as well as it did
was also due considerably to his inspiration, for battles are
often as much a matter of morale—and quick, calm thinking—as of armaments. The human element counts for
more than might be imagined.

After the persistent pummelling they received, the
Germans had no stomach for further fighting—or for
lunch! The last straw came when the look-out aboard
their battleship sighted through the mists the shadowy
silhouettes of heavier British ships rushed to the scene by
radio.

"Achtung!" he shouted, terror-stricken. If destroyers
did this to them, what would warships of the same size as
the German's manage? Not waiting to find out, they turned
a complete circle and raced back for the sanctuary of their
bases on the north Norwegian coast. They were only a few
hours out, so they could scarcely fail to make port. Once
there, they nursed their wounds and admitted that a
destroyer of the *Maas*-class had been lost. Admiralty
claimed damage to one of the two heavier enemy vessels—
and also regretted to have to announce the loss of H.M.
Destroyer *Achates*, under Lieutenant Commander A. H.
Tyndall Jones. She was damaged in the defence of the
convoy and then subsequently sunk.

The fantastic fact which will remain to Captain Sherbrooke's eternal credit is that the complete convoy got
through to Russia with its vital military supplies for the
Eastern front—unscathed by a bullet or a single shell. The
First Lord of the Admiralty said of the achievement that
there had "never been anything finer in naval annals."

Despite all the doctors' efforts, Captain Sherbrooke lost

the sight of his eye. He returned to active service a year later—to his first 'shore' appointment for twenty-seven years! He took over the command of one of the largest naval air stations in Britain. So he was still serving, with a glass eye as memento of that Arctic morning which ended 1942.

This, however, is not the end of Sherbrooke's story. After the War, the other side of the struggle at North Cape came to light in the German Admiral Raeder's speech on his retirement. At a conference on December 31, 1942—the day before the battle, notice—Goering was present when Hitler began talking of the superiority of the British Navy, and described the German one as "but a copy of the British and a very poor one at that." He said that the German ships were not in operational readiness, and lying idle in the fiords of Norway, utterly useless like so much old iron.

At that very moment, Admiral Krancke read a tele-typed message from the Operations Division that a German surface force was in contact with a British convoy off the North Cape. At the evening conference no more news had come in, but Hitler was promised reports the second they arrived, for, as Krancke said, "I know he cannot sleep a wink when ships are operating."

Next day Hitler became impatient, despite Krancke explaining the exigencies of radio silence. Hitler suggested they ask the task force for a very brief report by wireless, but Raeder refused to order ships to break radio silence.

Noon next day brought no news. It seemed a bad start to the New Year, and the Fuehrer became restless and ranted about the failure of the German Navy. Then that evening they heard the result of Operation Rainbow, as the Germans had called it. The destroyer *Friedrich Eckoldt* sunk; *Hipper* damaged and her speed reduced; only one British destroyer sunk; and the convoy continued!

The Fuehrer was furious.

"This is typical of German ships," he roared. "Just the opposite of the British who, true to their tradition, fought to the bitter end. The whole thing spells the end of the German High Seas Fleet," he went on.

Raeder was told of Hitler's decision to put most of the German surface navy out of commission, apart from a few ships for training. An amazing decision this was. As Raeder observed, the fleet was to all intents and purposes scuttled. Raeder failed to get a reprieve for the surface ships—and resigned. Doenitz, the U-boat admiral, took his place.

From these highest German sources, therefore, comes the evidence that Sherbrooke's superb Arctic action resulted directly in the immobilization of the entire enemy surface fleet.

No one man could hope to do more than that.

15

JOHN WALLACE LINTON

COMMANDER LINTON was the last of the three great submariners to be recognized with the V.C. Following in the
wake of Wanklyn and "Tony" Miers—who was under his
guidance, as we shall see later on—John Wallace Linton
proved as great as either of them. A tremendous trio these
men made. 'Tubby' Linton, as he was known to his
friends, actually sank as large a tonnage of enemy shipping as Wanklyn, that is, about one-eighth of a million
tons.

Tubby Linton was born at Malpas, near Newport in
Monmouthshire, though he was not Welsh. After Osborne
and Dartmouth, his next few years were to be remarkable
particularly for one thing more than all else—rugby football. He was 'capped' half a dozen times for the Navy between 1927 and 1930, and played, too, for Hampshire and
the United Services.

In the scrapbook which his mother kept of all his rugger
matches, one early one in 1927 made a memorable impression on Sub-Lieutenant Linton, as he then was. Before a
large crowd at Twickenham he was one of the forwards in
the winning Royal Navy team who beat the Royal Air
Force (the junior service!) by eight points to three.

In the loose rushes, Eyres, Linton, Harry, and Osborne
carried all before them. But—as a report of the match

makes clear—"the only new man who is likely to be considered seriously is J. W. Linton of the Navy. He certainly played well enough for any team; he is a hard worker, and of the right type for an International game."

So it went on. "Linton was the outstanding member of the pack." "Linton took his full share . . . in the many desperate situations that arose." "Linton was magnificent." Eventually he got an International trial but for some reason never an actual cap. As one of his friends has said of his game: "He could, and did, play with equal facility in any position in the scrum, which is something of a rarity in modern rugger."

For much of those years from '27 to '30, Linton played at home on the tree-lined United Services ground in Portsmouth, or away throughout the country. Perhaps the culminating occasion of his rugger life was the last big match of the season in 1930, when United Services brought off a vivid victory over Rosslyn Park by twenty points to six. The scores were level at the interval, but Services piled on the pressure afterwards, and their forwards broke through more than once to bring the total points to twenty. And the best of all these forwards? John Linton who was "prominent in attack and defence."

Well might this phrase be used again to sum up Linton's later life in command of the submarine *Turbulent*. First, attack. Then, defend his ship against counter-attack from 250 depth charges which were aimed at her.

But all that comes later. During the 'thirties, he had a couple of spells out East, far from the green turf and green-painted stand of the United Services ground. He served in H-class and L-class subs., and the two at Hong Kong were *Oberon* and *Oswald*. Out East it was that John Linton and his wife Nancy first knew Tony Miers, whose exploit in H.M. Submarine *Torbay* has already been told. In Hong Kong they also met Ryder of St Nazaire fame. These proved peaceful years, interspersed only by a brief patrol period, forming part of a commission back at Gibraltar. Here his submarine was on hand off the Spanish coast during the Civil War in that country: Linton's first association with war.

Soon, however, came 1939. By this time, John Linton had grown a great black beard. One trip from Hong Kong he had sailed clean-shaven, but when his submarine slipped back into that huge harbour with its encircling hills—he had the beard!

In the early years of the war he sailed his submarine *Pandora* to New Hampshire, U.S.A., for a refit, and came back to Britain to build the *Turbulent*. From then on the name of the ship might be applied to Linton's life. When it was completed, at Barrow-in-Furness, in January 1942, he took it straight into the fray—after the initial proving trials, of course. He sailed her down to the Mediterranean: not to Gibraltar or Malta, but the Eastern Med. around Alexandria and the Levant.

Only a month or so after the submarine's commissioning came news of her first success. On February 27, 1942, she sank a small 60-ton motor craft, rapidly following this on the 2nd and 3rd of March during the same patrol with four schooners sunk and one damaged.

Now in his late 'thirties, Commander John Wallace Linton was much older than many of his fellow commanders of subs. Wanklyn, for instance, was seven or eight years younger. He proved fighting fit for the arduous life led submerged beneath the Mediterranean surface. Sailing the sea-bed, or prowling at periscope depth, Linton left a trail of enemy ships strewn across his course. His record began to look like the long list of successes which Wanklyn had chalked up.

One night in a mixture of mist and moonlight, Tubby Linton (his weight was down now from the seventeen stone region to about fourteen) took the *Turbulent* up to a strong convoy consisting of two merchantmen and two destroyers. He watched it from afar at periscope depth before diving with the intention of attacking as the ships crossed the splintered line of reflected moonlight on the water. He brought *Turbulent* up again to periscope depth, grabbed hold of the hand-grips, swung the sights round, peered in—and saw one of the two destroyers almost on top of *Turbulent*. He smacked his lips, kept to his course, then called:

"Fire One."

One, then another, torpedo streaked through the night sea. The first struck and sank the other destroyer. More torpedoes accounted for the two merchantmen. Linton dived deep as the destroyer overhead counter-attacked. By skilful handling he managed to bring the sub. clear.

And so it went on: audacity and skill, hand in hand. An Italian destroyer, a U-boat, a German armed merchant cruiser were added to the list of ships he had sunk. Out of 365 days in the year since the start of the campaign, 254 days were spent at sea, nearly half that time submerged: thus he lived one-third of his life underwater! Coupling this to his previous service in the war, it is likely that by now he held the world's record for operational time in submarines.

Back at base he was always impatient to get into the battle, and passed his hours on depot ships talking over tactics with other submariners. On and on he went until the *Turbulent* could claim: one armed cruiser, one destroyer, one U-boat, twenty-eight supply ships mostly bound for North Africa and Rommel's army. All these sunk by a man who was quiet, reserved, but determined. He had no time for small talk.

Now it was spring, 1943. Linton wore the D.S.O. and the D.S.C. At home in Gloucestershire his wife kept the decorations safely in their cases: the D.S.O. with its white cross; green, red, and gold centrepiece; red and blue ribbon—the D.S.C. with its silver cross; blue and white striped ribbon. The D.S.C. he had received in person from H.M. George VI at an investiture.

Yet in addition to all these ships sunk, *Turbulent* claimed several other more unusual 'kills.' On the copy of the sub.'s Jolly Roger flag are the following insignia:

White bars for enemy ships sunk.

White U for the U-boat.

Red bar for the Italian destroyer.

Eight stars around crossed guns represent each success-ful gun action against enemy shipping.

And the unusual operations: a locomotive, a lorry, and a rail van with a streak across it are for gun actions against various forms of enemy shore transport. Three times *Turbulent* surfaced near enemy coasts and shot up a goods train, road convoy, and an electric train (represented by the streak of lightning).

She lay offshore in daylight once at periscope depth. Linton watched up-coast as the goods train chugged slowly along the sea-side line. Waiting till it was only a mile or so off the point in the track perpendicular to the position of the sub., he surfaced. Visibility was moderate. The engine driver did not see the sub. Neither did any coast defences, the area was wild. Suddenly the sub.'s gun cracked out across the water and an exploding shell told of a train shot from the rails in its very own country.

More intriguing still are two daggers for operations which even now cannot be revealed.

Linton refused to be relieved of underwater duties, and it was with a heavy heart that he sailed from port on his last scheduled patrol. After it he was due to be sent home for a rest earned a dozen times over. But on May 4, 1943, the world heard that *Turbulent* had failed to return to base and must be presumed lost on patrol. The last known of her was when she was sailing close to a minefield between Corsica and Sardinia, and the rest can be imagined. Through no conceivable fault of his own, Linton was lost —on his last trip.

But before this, on March 26, the Admiralty had sent a most secret cypher to Commander-in-Chief, Mediterranean, repeated to Commander-in-Chief, Levant. It would be wrong to reproduce more—or less—than this signal:

> It is with the deepest regret that their Lordships have learnt of the loss of *Turbulent* with the presumption of the death of Commander J. W. Linton. In view of very special and distinguished services of this officer, who has been in command of S/Ms throughout the whole period of this war and whose outstanding characteristics and achievements were so well known throughout the Mediterranean commands, they wish to express their sympathy to you and to the Mediterranean S/M Flotillas.
>
> Their Lordships do so with assurance that Commander Linton's inspiring leadership will long be remembered by all those who are so worthily upholding the traditions of the Royal Navy and the submarine service in the Mediterranean at the present time.

On May 25, 1943, the Victoria Cross was awarded to the late Commander Linton. Nancy Linton later received it. And as she opened the case and saw the plain purple ribbon and simple bronze cross, she remembered many things. She and her mother then wrote personal letters to all the next of kin of those who were lost with Linton.

She remembered how he hated any 'line-shooting' and how the press sensationalized his exploits. He had to have accuracy, too. As she sat alone she smiled to herself as one occasion in a cinema came to her mind. A newsreel of a submarine diving was accompanied by a commentary which told the audience that the whole diving operation took three to four minutes.

"Fifty seconds," Tubby Linton muttered into his beard.

Nancy Linton also received a letter from Tony Miers. It was far more eloquent in its sincerity than a lifetime of biographical detail, and she has always kept it. Writing from mid-ocean aboard U.S.S. *Cabrilla*, Captain Anthony Miers wrote:

MY DEAR MRS "TUBBY,"

I have only recently heard the awful news and don't know what I can say to express to you my sorrow. I got a letter from Admiral Barry just before leaving for patrol (in my capacity as liaison officer) and now at sea there is time and quiet to sit down to this unhappy task; but it won't be posted for so long and will reach you so late that I fear it will re-open an old wound. At the same time as getting the letter, I received a copy of the A.F.O. (Admiralty Fleet Order) with the citation for the Victoria Cross in it. What magnificent reading it made and how absolutely true every word of it and how very proud you must be. Of course, a decoration is no substitute for Tubby, but what a wonderful and glorious climax to a brilliant career and what a terrific example for not only his boys to follow but for all of us. I can't begin to tell you how much I personally shall miss him—he was always a very staunch friend, when I was the junior 1st Lieut. in China and he the senior one; when I joined the "Iron Duke" as a stranger to big ships and boys' training; and when I arrived out in the Mediterranean for the first time since I was a midshipman for my first war patrol with a new boat. Tubby taught me everything and gave me tips that no one else would bother to do, and if they did, they had not the ability to impart the knowledge as he had. And when I got my decoration I felt then that he should have had it, as he was the mainspring and inspiration of the whole flotilla out there—not me. And I owed so very much to his patience and wisdom. Also I had such a short spell compared to his, and he would have been so *much* better at this job than me. He was such a master of his trade and I am by no means anything of the sort.

There is no point in my saying any more—you know what we all feel about his loss and I just had to write and tell you how very deeply I sympathize with you and your sons.

On the lighter side there will be so many happy memories to cherish; of bowls games in China, of rugger matches everywhere, of many wardroom arguments and bridge games (which he always won) and in particular one lovely battle in the "Iron Duke" over who was to pay for some champagne that the Navigator organized for Captain Phillips' wedding anniversary without authority in the Mess. I shall never forget Tubby saying to the Parson, who was calling us mean for not agreeing to the Mess paying, "All right, next week is *my* wedding anniversary and, of course, there will be champagne down to the Mess."

And another time when the same navigator insisted on taking over on the bridge for an alteration of course when Tubby was officer of the watch. So Tubby went down to the Wardroom and drank gin and refused to go back as he had been relieved. The navigator was left "holding the baby." In future he always let Tubby alter course by himself, which as a Submarine C.O. he was very capable of doing. These and a thousand other memories of his forceful personality and yet infinite kindness of heart I shall always treasure.

I must stop this long effusion now but I have 'got it off my chest' and only hope the New Year will bring you better fortune and that you and your boys are well and flourishing.

Yours

TONY MIERS

At that time the boys were flourishing. But William Francis was later commissioned and served in 1951 on the last journey of H.M. Submarine *Affray*, thus following in his father's footsteps.

16

DONALD CAMERON
BASIL CHARLES GODFREY PLACE

So far five submariners had won the V.C., all operating in conventional craft. But four more V.C.s were won in those astonishing little brothers to the larger submarines—the midget subs. The first two of them were won in the now famous attack on the German battleship *Tirpitz* as she was moored in the protected waters of Kaafiord, Northern Norway.

The date of the attack was September 22, 1943, but the story of the midget subs., or X-craft as they were called, started eighteen months earlier—or four years and more if their design and development is taken into account as well.

The first X-craft was launched, however, just about a year and a half before the culminating *Tirpitz* triumph. It took the water on the Hamble, a river flowing into the Solent near Southampton, on March 15, 1942, while the assault parties for the St Nazaire raid were commencing their training further westward along the south coast. Lieutenant Donald Cameron, later to command one of the midgets in the *Tirpitz* attack, was one of the crew of three.

The X-craft was like a submarine but on a smaller scale. Her overall length came to about fifty feet, but the propeller, rudder, and hydroplanes came within this figure so that the actual area internally measured a mere thirty-five feet. The diameter of the pressure-hull at its greatest point was five and a half feet, but the wooden deck boards took the odd half a foot, so that only five feet remained as headroom.

For'ard was the control-room, with the steering gear and controls for keeping to the correct depth; the all-important periscope, the only eyes the men would have whilst underwater, and a miscellany of navigation aids and other machinery.

Aft of the control room came the escape compartment. This 'wet and dry' chamber (as it was known) enabled one member of the crew actually to leave the submarine in diving equipment to cut anti-submarine nets or to place particular explosive charges—and then return to the sub. Aft again were battery compartment and engine and motor spaces.

It was not normally necessary to place explosives in the way described, though, as the vessel's main armament consisted of two 'side-cargoes' accommodated outside the hull. These contained a couple of tons of Amatol each and a time-clock which could be set from within the submarine. Upon release, the side-cargoes would drop quietly to the sea-bed beneath the ship being attacked, and explode after a sufficient time to allow the midget to make its getaway.

The diesel engine used when the sub. was surfaced gave her a speed of $6\frac{1}{2}$ knots. The battery-driven main motor operating while she proceeded underwater produced $4\frac{1}{2}$ knots.

Through the autumn and winter of 1941–42 trials had continued slowly but satisfactorily, and in October the first two side-cargoes had been released and exploded experimentally. The volume of water upswept into the air above the peace of Itchenor harbour, Sussex, certainly bode ill for any enemy ships which might later find similar charges going off under them. The X-craft looked like the

answer to attacking such ships as *Tirpitz* where normal
submarines could never penetrate, because of their size
and the protective nets. Surrounding the fiord where
Tirpitz was eventually attacked, moreover, the high hills
made an air attack out of the question. So it was up to the
midget subs. to stop the manœuvres of this great German
ship, whose mere presence meant keeping British ships on
hand near the North Sea when they could be better employed safeguarding the convoys across the Atlantic—
which were still suffering such heavy losses from U-boats.

The legendary Sir Max Horton visited X3 in January
1942, about the time when the 'wet and dry' compartment was receiving its full trials.

On March 15, 1942, the official launching was conducted—at 11 p.m., for secrecy. Under her own power she
moved away from the bank of the Hamble. Full-scale
trials went ahead rapidly. She was 'wiped,' or degaussed,
against magnetic mines, she passed her surface trials, and
then her diving tests.

Late in April three more 'recruits' to the ranks of
midget sub. crew included Midshipman John Lorimer,
later to attack the *Tirpitz* with Cameron. He was shown
over X3 by Cameron, and wondered at first how such a
small craft could possibly cross the North Sea to so remote
a spot as the fiords frequented by *Tirpitz*. More volunteers
joined in July and August—twenty-five in two months.
The tests went on and on—tests on the men as well as the
sub. Security was vital. X3 was only sailed inshore after
dark.

Meanwhile trials took most of the summer: mock
attacks on Portland Harbour, and many others. The sub.
was still in an early stage of development really, however,
and unforeseen things could easily happen.

A year before the successful *Tirpitz* raid, another attempt was made by those other little underwater craft—

the human torpedoes. Two men actually sat abreast the *outside* of these remarkable craft, called Chariots. Unfortunately this attempt failed. Two of the Chariots were towed by a "Norwegian fishing vessel" which actually contained the crews, but only ten miles from the *Tirpitz*, in rough weather, they broke loose and sank. However, the British naval men and their Norwegian guide, Leif Larsen, of the Royal Norwegian Navy's Special Service Unit, managed to get back to Britain, so all was not lost.

At last, in September 1943, all the months of training for the crews of X-craft were over, and the midgets prepared to tackle *Tirpitz*: a thousand miles of rough seas to an objective protected by every conceivable device to destroy any sort of vessel which might venture near. *Tirpitz* herself lay no less than sixty miles from the sea, close under cliffs at the head of Kaafiord.

The overall plan included attacks on the 26,000-ton *Scharnhorst* and 12,000-ton *Lutzow* as well as the main prize, the 40,000-ton *Tirpitz*. Eighteen months' training over, six steel X-craft set out on their mission. They were towed by submarines most of the way, and passage-crews in the midgets spent a tiring eight days seeing them safely across the North Sea and up towards Northern Norway. Two men out of the three in each of the midgets had to remain on watch for most of the twenty-four hours. Four times each day the little craft surfaced for a quarter of an hour, while keeping submerged for the other twenty-three hours. The operational crews, including Cameron and Lieutenant Godfrey Place, meanwhile, got more fresh air as the full-size subs. steamed on the surface all night.

Final orders received on the fifth day out told X5, X6, and X7 to attack *Tirpitz*; X8 to go for *Lutzow*; and X9 and X10 to aim at *Scharnhorst*. Until now all had been quiet, but the receipt of them seemed to step-up the suspense and to coincide with the first difficulties.

At the worst possible time, 0400, the bows of X8 suddenly swung downward, showing that her tow had most probably parted from her big brother sub., *Seanymph*. Within five minutes Lieutenant J. E. Smart, in command, surfaced the midget raider, clambered on to her casing, and looked round. No sign of *Seanymph*. Smart decided to plod along the surface at three knots and hope to be found.

Seanymph did not discover the parted tow until a couple of hours later. The sub. was swung round to retrace her course, but after a six-hours' search in rough sea, she found nothing.

Meanwhile, X8 had located and lost again the submarine *Stubborn*, towing X7. The cause this time was that a course had been wrongly heard in the fury of wind and sea. Although *Stubborn* lost contact with X8 she did see *Seanymph*, and thus was able to let her know the approximate position of the latter's small sister. At 1700 hours, after a day and a half, *Seanymph* and her charge were reunited. Smart spent practically all those hours on his feet, and the operational crew took over.

Next morning at 0900, *Syrtis* fired the usual underwater exploding signals to tell her small craft to surface. No response. At 0920 they hauled in the tow, which was found to have parted. *Syrtis* carried out an exhaustive search for hour after hour, but none of the towing submarines ever saw X9 again. The midget *Syrtis* had been towing became the first X-craft lost on operations. What surely happened was that the tiny sub. sailed trimmed heavy at the bow to offset the upward pull of the tow from the big sub. The tow suddenly snapped. The bow took the extra weight of the heavy rope—and the sub. was swept down too deep before compensating action to balance her could be taken. Her sides would have caved in and the water pressure have proved fatal. The passage crews had a job just as dangerous as the operational crews.

The next craft to get into difficulties was X8, whose
trim seemed to be all wrong, and who was hard to handle.
At last the main ballast tanks were called in correct trim.
The trouble was traced to an air-leak from the buoyancy
chambers to starboard. With the trim still extremely difficult to maintain, Lieutenant B. M. McFarlane, R.A.N.,
decided to get rid of the starboard explosive charge. The
depth of water here was 180 fathoms, and this side-cargo
was set 'safe,' in other words not to explode. Fifteen
minutes later, however, it went off with a very big bang
only 1000 yards astern of the midget. Neither X8 nor
Seanymph suffered any harm, but X8 was certainly keeping
up a reputation for unpredictability.

Despite jettisoning the starboard charge, trim remained
hard to control, and eventually the port side-cargo had to
go, too, much to the disappointment of the crew.

Distrusting the 'safe' setting of the first charge, the
C.O.s decided to fire this one after a two-hour delay.
Although the two subs. were nearly four miles away when
it went off, the impact of the explosion inside the midget
proved far worse than the first. The 'wet and dry' chamber
was flooded, doors distorted, pipes fractured, and the craft
altogether made useless for further operations. The crew
were taken on board *Seanymph*, and X8 was scuttled so
that she should not be on the surface and endanger the
rest of the operation. The only change in the plan as a
result was that the *Lutzow* would not now be able to be
attacked.

By dusk on September 18 the weather relented a little
and Godfrey Place took Lieutenant "Bill" Whittam and
the rest of the operational crew aboard X7. The change-
over occurred outside Altenfiord, and Place borrowed the
passage-crew C.O.'s best boots, fur-lined and leather.

The other three submarines waited until the next day
before they transferred operational crews. *Thrasher* was

towing X5; *Truculent*, X6; and *Sceptre*, X10: 5, 6, 7, 10; the other two were gone.

The crews had been transferred a night ahead of schedule, but still the midgets were being towed, though. The plan was for them to make their attacks and return to the big brother subs.

Truculent, *Thrasher*, and *Sceptre* towed their X-craft. *Syrtis* had none. *Stubborn* would arrive soon with X7. *Syrtis* sighted a U-boat at less than a mile but could not attack it—by order. They did not want to attract any attention, however tempting a target came into view. All of them, moreover, managed to keep out of sight all this way.

Later that day, *Stubborn* sighted a mine with its mooring rope caught in the tow of X7. The deadly weapon came right along the line of the hawser until it reached the bows of X 7. Place crawled along the casing of the midget and untangled it from the hawser and bows with his feet, while all the time it bobbed about on the Arctic waters. Sweat streamed down his face despite the cold. At last he managed to push it clear of the X-craft, by clever kicks on its shell *between* the lethal-looking horns.

Early evening on September 20 the four little craft slipped their tows and left their guardians, who withdrew out to sea. Thus the midgets made their way into the Soroy Sound just about the ordered time, after nine difficult, dangerous days.

From this point onward, the two X's bound for the *Tirpitz*—6 and 7—kept pretty well together without ever encountering each other. The starboard charge of X6 had been flooded since the very first day of the tow, but by stowing the stores and spare equipment slightly differently, the craft kept a good enough trim.

Both craft crossed the minefield off Soroy during the night of September 20–21. *Tirpitz* would be coming within striking distance soon. They proceeded up the Altenfiord during daylight on the 21st. Cameron's periscope on X6 developed a defect, but the danger of 'blindness' passed. As she crawled up the fiord at periscope depth, X7 saw several enemy vessels during the day. Fortunately visibility was fairly good, and Place could dive the sub. in time to avoid being seen. Even the tell-tale periscope trail at that stage could still ruin the whole operation if it were noticed, but no one did notice anything so unusual as a pair of midget subs. picking a steady course straight for the pride of the German Navy. En route, in the lee of Aaroy Island, about tea-time, Place was tempted by the sight of the *Scharnhorst* close to X7. His orders were to attack *Tirpitz*, so all he could do was to swing his periscope away from so beckoning a target and remember the one a little further on, half as big again.

On the port side of the fiord lay the Brattholm group of islands, and here at 70° North X6 and X7 spent the night of the 21st–22nd. X10 arrived later. X6 had to dive during the night on more than one occasion as she lay very near to the shipping lane to Hammerfest. X7, too, had some narrow squeaks as she tried to charge batteries and small boats chugged to and fro only a mile or so off. It would be heartbreaking if anything went wrong so near *Tirpitz*. The only other excitement of the night was Engine Room Artificer Whitley's successful efforts to fit a spare exhaust pipe—which he finally managed with the assistance of sticky tape and chewing gum!

At last they reached the final fiord. They had negotiated all Altenfiord. Soon after midnight, X7 left the lee of the Brattholm's for Kaafiord, off the head of the longer waterway. X6 followed one hour afterwards.

The first—and a foremost—obstacle loomed upon them quickly: the anti-submarine net at the entrance of the fiord; a metal mesh, reaching almost to the bottom of this inland sea so far from the real sea. But they were ready for it. Place got X7 through the net, but Cameron had more difficulty. His periscope had begun to flood soon after leaving the islands, and time and time again it did this, so that Cameron could scarcely see anything up top. He made out the watery shape of a small coaster about to go through the net. This 'boom' had just been opened to let the vessel through, so he daringly surfaced and put on all possible speed. X6 actually swept through the anti-submarine net at early light of morning in the wake of the enemy coaster! The sub's size—or lack of it—was certainly an advantage.

Once through the net, Cameron dived to sixty feet and sailed by dead reckoning. He stripped the periscope but still it was imperfect. Hardly surprising was it, therefore, that X6 only barely avoided head-on collisions. Once she passed just beneath the bows of a stationary destroyer; another time up, Cameron found her heading straight for the mooring buoy of a tanker half a mile from *Tirpitz*. Not a sound nor a ripple must disturb the scene now. The waters of Kaafiord were glass-still. E. R. A. Goddard had to keep all his wits about him on the wheel of X6. By 0705, X6 had reached the anti-torpedo shore-net defence of *Tirpitz* and was through the boat entrance.

Meanwhile, X7 had been forced deep by a patrolling launch and been caught in a square of anti-torpedo nets once used to protect the *Lutzow*, but now no longer needed. For an hour or more before dawn Place pumped and blew until the craft at last shook herself free and shot up to the surface. Then a single strand of wire hooked itself across the periscope standard. By 0600 this came clear, and Place set course up-fiord for the target.

By 0710, X7 reached the anti-torpedo net defences. Place tried to negotiate these by diving to 75 feet—but was caught. While she began to try and extricate herself, X6 followed a picket boat through the boat gate. Breakfast was being prepared aboard the *Tirpitz* in blissful ignorance of the double danger so near at hand.

In calm, shallow water, X6 ran gently aground. She managed to free herself, but for the first time they started a stir in *Tirpitz*; for in freeing the craft from the bottom they broke surface for a few seconds. A look-out aboard the battleship spotted them and reported "a long submarine-like object." His senior thought it might be a porpoise and delayed passing the report on for five vital minutes. X6 was now inside the range of *Tirpitz*'s main and secondary guns. Again, just as the message had been conveyed to an officer, X6 struck a rock and broke surface. She was identified, but before she could be fired on Lorimer swung her down again. She was a mere eighty yards abeam of the battleship, but the gyro was out of action and the periscope almost fully flooded. All Cameron could do was to try to fix their position by the shadow of the battleship.

Yet another five hectic minutes passed. X6 became tangled in an obstruction hanging down from the *Tirpitz* herself. To wriggle clear, she had to surface once more— to the accompaniment of strong small-arms fire and hand grenades tossed from the deck of *Tirpitz*. Cameron knew that escape was out of the question now. With the vast armament the battleship carried and all the other auxiliary vessels in the fiord, X6 could never get away.

"Smash all the secret equipment," he ordered, in case the Germans salvaged the craft. "I'm going to scuttle her."

Cameron took X6 astern till the hydroplane guard was touching *Tirpitz*'s hull, and released the two charges, set to fire one hour later. Then the time was 0715. He scuttled the craft and they bailed out in turn through the wet and dry compartment.

In a matter of seconds they were struggling in the water

near *Tirpitz*. The German ship put out a picket boat and picked them up, and also made a vain attempt to slip a tow around X6 as she sank.

'Action stations' had been sounded aboard *Tirpitz*, and from the state of unreadiness it was all too clear that complete surprise had been achieved. (This took twenty minutes; the slowness with which the Germans prepared to shift the ship was unbelievable.) All watertight doors were closed. Then steam for the boilers was ordered. While steam still was not up to pressure for sailing, divers went over the side to see if they could trace the charges laid on the bottom.

Cameron, Lorimer, Goddard, and Sub-Lieutenant "Dick" Kendall stood in a group to one side while orders went to and fro. No one interrogated them yet, but they had been given hot coffee and schnapps after their icy dip.

Cameron glanced down at his watch surreptitiously. It was eight o'clock. Only a quarter of an hour before the charges were due off. Things had not gone quite according to plan, of course, for they were not meant to be aboard *Tirpitz* on the receiving end of their own charges. They shifted a trifle restlessly from one foot to the other.

Meanwhile X7 had stuck in the net at 75 feet depth— no picnic place, as they knew that X6's charge would fire any time after 0800. Place decided they must get clear as soon as humanly possible. He blew the tanks to full buoyancy and steamed full astern. She came out, but turned beam on to the net and broke surface. Then he dived quickly.

The boat stuck by the bow. The depth this time was 95 feet. After five minutes of wriggling and blowing, she started to rise. The compass had gone haywire. Place did not know how near the shore he was. He stopped the motor, and X7 came up to the surface. Amazingly, she must have passed underneath the nets or through the boat gate, for Place now saw *Tirpitz* straight ahead—thirty yards off.

"Forty feet . . . full speed ahead . . ."

She struck *Tirpitz* on her port side and slid quietly under the keel. Place released the starboard charge.

"Sixty feet . . . slow astern . . ."

The port charge was released 150–200 feet further aft.

It was 0730 now and X6 had been scuttled. Place ordered 100 feet depth for X7 and guessed the position they had got through the net, for the compass still would not work. At 60 feet they were in the net again. Air was getting short now. Their charges would go off about 0830, and X6's any time after 0800. The situation became urgent.

X7 became entangled amongst first one net, and another, and another. At 0740, her crew extricated her from one by sliding over the top of the net between the surface buoys. Luckily they were too close for heavy fire from *Tirpitz*, but they were peppered with machine-gun bullets which hammered against the casing.

After passing over the nets, they at once dived again— to 120 feet and the bottom. Once more they tried to surface or reach periscope to see where they were and so be able to get as far as possible from the forthcoming bangs, which could easily prove fatal to the midget. But in so doing, they ran into yet another net at sixty feet and, frantically frustrated, tried to get clear.

Back aboard *Tirpitz*, divers returned to the vessel, having examined the hull for limpet mines stuck to the ship.

Cameron slipped his sleeve up a fraction.

"It's 0810," he breathed to Lorimer.

Then they were summoned to questioning and asked what charges they had placed—and where.

Still the ship had not moved. All but an hour had

passed. They stalled their answers, praying, too, that the ship would not sail clear of the explosions.

0811: they prayed again that they were not directly over the charges.

0812: a shattering explosion from the bowels of the fiord below the boat.

They were thrown off their feet by the force of it. Their own four tons of amatol had also sent up X7's four tons. Eight tons of explosive were tearing into the *Tirpitz*.

There was complete panic aboard. The German gun-crew shot up some of their own tankers and small boats, and obliterated a shore position. The chaos was un-believable. About a hundred men were lost, mainly through their own lack of self-control.

True, *Tirpitz* still floated, but with the force of the explosion the great ship heaved five or six feet upward and at once listed five degrees to port. A huge column of water streamed into the air on the port side and fell on to the decks. All the lights failed, and oil-fuel started to leak out from midships. Much more damage was obviously done.

The surge of the explosion cracked through the water to X7, shaking her clear of the net. Place took her to the surface, saw *Tirpitz* still afloat, then dived deep again. Her crew gathered themselves together and took stock of the damage. Compasses and depth gauges out of order, but little wrong structurally. Nevertheless the craft could not be controlled, and broke surface several times. Each time she did so, *Tirpitz* fired on them, denting and damaging the hull more.

Place decided to abandon ship and brought the craft to the surface. They could not use the escape chambers from a submerged position as depth-charges were being dropped which might have killed them while ascending from the craft. She surfaced close to a gunnery target, but before the crew could get out of the control-room, the

gunfire sank her. Place was up on the casing, however, so
stepped clear to the gunnery target—to be picked up and
taken aboard *Tirpitz*.

At about that moment, at 0843, X5 was sighted 500
yards outside the nets. *Tirpitz* opened fire and claimed to
have sunk her. Depth-charges were dropped, too, and
nothing was ever heard of the third X-craft to get within
sight of *Tirpitz*.

Back in X7, it was a matter of life and death for the
next two or three hours. After diving for the last time she
struck the bottom within seconds. Luckily the hatch had
been shut in time. Bill Whittam took over. The diving
escape sets were cut down from the stowage spot. Whittam
began to flood the ship. There was no panic. They decided
to use both escape hatches. Lieutenant Whittam and
E. R. A. Whitley would use one each, and Sub-Lieutenant
Aitken whichever one was clear first. But they could not
pass each other with their escape gear on, so Aitken was
left by the 'wet and dry' hatch for'ard.

Flooding was frighteningly slow, nor could it be speeded
up. The icy cold water rose gradually up their bodies, then
fused an electric circuit—and the craft filled with fumes.
They breathed their escape-oxygen. With the boat about
fully flooded, Aitken tried the for'ard hatch, but it would
not open.

He climbed back into the control-room and found that
Whitley had slipped. Aitken groped under the water to
find that the breathing-bag was flat and the two emergency
cylinders had been consumed. Whitley was dead.

In the darkness Aitken started to try and find Bill
Whittam—but as he straightened up his own oxygen
bottle gave out, too. In a flash, he broke open the two
emergency-oxylets, which at that depth gave him only a
breath or two each. He was very nearly dead, his last
oxygen-reserves gone, in a flooded submarine at 120 feet

with two men, both presumably dead, and the hatch still shut. All he had left in life was the breath he was still holding in his lungs. He scrambled somehow back into the escape compartment for a last lunge at the hatch. Then he blacked out—till he opened his eyes to see a stream of oxygen bubbles as he sped to the surface. He must have managed to open the hatch and done his escape drill in a dream.

At 1115, Bob Aitken broke surface. A few minutes later he was drinking coffee and schnapps, wrapped in a German blanket. He sat shivering still, remembering Whittam and Whitley.

Later it was learned that all three main engines of the *Tirpitz* were put out of action; a generator room; all lighting and electrical equipment; wireless telegraphy rooms; hydrophone station; A and C turrets; anti-aircraft control positions; range-finding gear; and the port rudder. The German naval war staff announced that she had been put out of action for months. Not until the following April was she able to limp from her anchorage, still crippled, only to be damaged and finally destroyed by air attack.

The six survivors of the X-craft attack were made prisoners of war. All were decorated, Cameron and Place with the V.C. Theirs had been "A magnificent feat of arms," as Sir Max Horton described it.

17

```
┌─────────────────────────────────────┐
│                                       │
│         THOMAS PECK HUNTER            │
│                                       │
└─────────────────────────────────────┘
```

AT last the Allies were on the offensive. Rommel was routed in North Africa, the battle of the Atlantic abated a little, Europe was being assaulted from all sides (east from Russia, north from Britain and France, now liberated, and south from Italy), and by the spring of 1945 the allied forces—land, sea, and air—moved northward through Italy. The Navy had played an important part in the original Sicilian and Italian invasions, the Army was on the move, and the Air Force was battering the enemy from above. In such a combined operation it is fitting that a V.C. commemorating this phase should have been awarded to a man combining the duties and qualities of more than one of the services.

He was the late Temporary Corporal Thomas Peck Hunter, Ch/X110296, of the Royal Marines, attached to special service troops. He won the award posthumously for gallantry during an advance of the 43rd Royal Marine Commando troops. Hunter had charge of a Bren gun group on the attack.

The wild, towering hills of Italy swept away into the distance. The valleys began to blossom. But the troops noticed none of this. The group got to within 400 yards of a canal and then halted for a minute. Suddenly Hunter saw strong enemy forces to the south holding a row of houses. In a flash he realized that his troop behind him would be bound to be exposed to withering fire from less than a quarter of a mile range, for much of the intervening ground lay open.

He seized a Bren gun, checked it for magazine in a moment, and hurled himself forward across 200 yards of flat open land to attract enemy fire on him and distract it from the rest of the troop. He ran at top speed, firing from the hip an incessant flow, so quickly that none of the enemy could hit him. They took one or two hasty aims, then all in a matter of seconds began to be demoralized— by one man.

A hundred yards from the houses, Hunter's first magazine gave out, but by this time he had started a surge of fear through the Germans. He was too close for their comfort. Quicker than he had ever changed magazines before, he ejected the used one and reloaded—firing afresh almost before the new magazine clicked home.

He was at the houses now, but the ordeal went on. Through them he ran at full speed, still firing—the stream of bullets sounding louder in the empty rooms.

As his boots thudded up to one landing, six Germans ran out to meet him, their hands high over their heads. The rest had already clattered away round the back of the houses and fled across a footbridge to the north bank of the canal.

He accepted the surrender of the six soldiers, motioning them to meet two or three of his troops advancing on the houses. He could wait no longer. Many men had to be got across that flat 400 yards, and the enemy could still fire on them from the north bank of the canal.

For a second time Hunter offered himself as a target. He rushed round to the south of the canal and flung himself flat on a heap of rubble. The Germans had reached a couple of concrete pillboxes. Hunter took out another magazine, slotted it into place in the black Bren gun, and ran his eyes along the sights. The gun gave him hardly any shelter. A frenzy of fire from the pillboxes turned on to him again. He returned it, accurately, unerringly. Several Germans succumbed and chips of concrete fell from their pillboxes. This was short-range war with a vengeance: the enemy near the north bank, Hunter on the south only a hundred yards away, and his troop advancing to the houses behind his holocaust of covering fire. The enemy never had a chance to set their sights on the troops for more than a moment. They decided their best chance was to concentrate on Hunter first—then go for his troops.

The troop tore towards the houses, where half of them remained. Still Hunter was firing from just off the crest of his heap of rubble. Two-thirds of the troop across to safety, though a few fell to the enemy fire.

Hunter felt for another magazine, but he had none. In that instant bullets burst over the rubble, hit him in the head, and he was killed.

Without his self-sacrifice, the troop would never have crossed that 400 yards, or if they had, their casualties would have been infinitely heavier.

18

IAN EDWARD FRASER
JAMES JOSEPH MAGENNIS

LIEUTENANT IAN EDWARD FRASER and Leading Seaman James Joseph Magennis won the Victoria Cross in Singapore Strait. A midget sub., XE3, was their craft, and noon, July 26, 1945, the time of departure for their attack on one of two 10,000-ton Japanese heavy cruisers, the *Nachi* and *Takao*, lying in the Johore Strait near Singapore Island.

Meanwhile the Japanese warships were at anchor, waiting to be attacked. Although they had not been to sea for some time, they were in a position to shell the Singapore Causeway across the Straits, which could have been dangerous to any Allied forces approaching the island by that route. XE1 would attack the *Nachi* and XE3, the subject of this chapter, the *Takao*.

Operational submarines towed the two XE's from their starting point, Brunei Bay, Borneo. H.M. Submarine *Stygian* towed XE3. Telephonic touch broke down, and the only means of communication between the 'parent' and 'child' was walkie-talkie sets used when the two submarines surfaced.

A passage crew occupied XE3 during the four days of the outward tow. They were lucky in having good weather, because, as the Commander-in-Chief of the British Pacific Fleet stressed afterwards, the task of the passage crew is a hard one: the towing speed at times reaches as much as eleven knots, yet all the while moisture has to be mopped up, and every scrap of equipment kept at 100 per cent. efficiency. The whole operation depends on their success. Needless to say, both XE1 and XE3 were turned over to the operational crews in perfect condition.

This change-over from the passage crew was effected at 0600 on the morning of July 30. Seventeen hours later, the tow was slipped at the dead of night, leaving XE3 alone at sea in a spot forty miles from the *Takao*'s anchorage.

Operation Struggle it had been named. Now the final phase of the struggle started. With the commander of XE3 (Ian Fraser) were Sub-Lieutenant W. J. L. (Kiwi) Smith of the Royal New Zealand Naval Volunteer Reserve, Engine Room Artificer Charles Reed, and Leading Seaman Mick Magennis. Fraser fortunately stood only five feet four inches, so was much happier upright in a midget sub.'s five and threequarter feet headroom than a man a foot taller! He had had plenty of practice, but this was his first X-craft operation.

Throughout the rest of that night he sat on the casing looking through binoculars, as the sub. slipped softly through the waters on the surface. He left the safe 'swept' channel on purpose, to avoid enemy listening posts, and navigated through a known minefield, thus avoiding the danger of being heard approaching.

In the very middle of the night, as he dangled his legs and looked through the glasses, he suddenly saw the dark outline of a tanker with an armed escort proceeding towards the Singapore Straits. He scrambled to his feet, vanished below, shut the 'lid' behind him, and uttered the one word: "Dive."

"The safest thing for us to do, Kiwi," he told the First Lieutenant, "is to sit on the bottom for as long as it takes this little Oriental procession to pass."

Thirty minutes later he came to periscope depth to

peep. They were safe from the ships, but not from the minefield; for only then did he notice that the craft had become entangled with a mine, which had not exploded.

By mid-morning on July 31, Fraser sighted the trawler which acted as guard-vessel at the submarine net-boom. Magennis was preparing his gear for 'baling out' quickly and cutting a way through the wire netting.

"Don't bother, Magennis," Fraser called. "It looks as if the 'gate' has been left open by some kind soul."

Even so, the navigational job was extremely difficult. Fraser had to take XE3 along the side of the guard-vessel, quite close to it, shifting the sub. at a snail's pace. The water was shallow, and the sun shone deep down almost to the bottom. The sub. slithered through the clear water, visible to any one who might have been looking down from the enemy ship. But no one was!

The first real hazard had been beaten, but worse was to come further along the route. Fraser navigated at periscope depth through several miles of narrow channels where a steady sea-traffic came and went. Keen pilotage from Fraser, level depth-keeping by Smith, and alert steering from Reed, was necessary.

A few minutes after noon Fraser said simply:

"There she is."

The *Takao* lay ahead, a very heavy cruiser carrying eight 8-inch guns—one shell from which would wipe out XE3.

He lowered periscope. It was not wise to keep it up for more than a second or so. Two hours passed and they got closer to the cruiser.

About 1400 hours, just after lunch on a scorching day, he went into the attack. He took a quick peep through the periscope—then dropped it at the double! Only a cricket-pitch of water away through the lens was a cutter full of

Japanese sailors—'liberty men' going ashore for the after-noon. XE3 dived. The cutter passed. Fraser continued blind. He knew where the cruiser lay, but not exactly how deep or shallow was the water. He wondered if he could get XE3 underneath her? As it transpired, *Takao* was in extremely shallow water for such a ship. XE3 went in with her keel scraping the bottom of the sea.

This was going to be difficult, the more so since the method of attack would be different from the *Tirpitz* attack. Even on the bed, Fraser could not find enough water. XE3 came to the cruiser's plating and hit it hard and true with a metallic thud. They wondered if the ship had heard it. Fraser brought the craft out astern again, and by a series of trials—and errors—he discovered that the Japanese ship lay almost aground at either end, but with some water under her amidships.

The clock ticked towards 1500. By plying back and forth parallel to the *Takao*, and occasionally hitting her hull, XE3 at last found a spot halfway under the cruiser, not a pleasant place to be, with ten thousand tons of enemy shipping on top. Fraser wedged XE3 between the hull and the sea-bed—although he knew that she might become more tightly squeezed if the tide fell much lower.

Magennis had the job of getting outside the craft on the bottom of enemy waters to attach limpet mines to the hull of the *Takao* which would go off in due course and hole her. He went into the chamber, flooded it, and then found that the external hatch only opened a quarter of the normal amount—only a matter of inches. He deflated the breathing apparatus, breathed out until his chest was as small as possible, and squeezed through the hatch. Then he began to unload the limpet charges from the port con-tainer on the outside of the sub.; but as he did so a stream of oxygen bubbles escaped from his equipment, which must have been damaged while he was wrestling with the hatch. Any one seeing them reach the surface would have at once become more than suspicious.

He took the first limpet mine from its container, and prepared to place it against the hull of the ship. It was supposed to stay there by magnetism, but the cruiser's hull was so thick with barnacles, and the ship lay at such a slope, that the magnets would not work. Magennis scraped a little patch free and then secured the charges in pairs. For half an hour he swam, scraped, carried, and tied, securing them with a line under the ship's keel. An exhausting job it was, far more so since his supply of oxygen slowly but steadily went on leaking.

He could well have placed just one or two, and then returned to XE3: he attached the entire half a dozen over a length of 45 feet of hull. He got back exhausted to the 'wet and dry' hatch, struggled through it, shut it, dried out the chamber, and collapsed into the control room. How he shut the hatch in his condition was a miracle, particularly as his hands had been torn to pieces with vicious lacerations from the barnacles. They brought him a drink and sat him down in a bunk, wrenching his diving apparatus off him.

XE3 had done its job. She could make her getaway. But still the hazards hung about her. All she had to do was get rid of the starboard side-cargo, the large explosive charge, and the port limpet-container—and back out. But *Takao* had closed her hold on the tiny adversary and would not let her free.

For nearly an hour XE3 went full astern, full ahead, and did everything conceivable to the tanks. But it was to no avail. It looked as if they would die as soon as the charges fired: killed with their own explosives. The waiting was nerve-racking. All of them sweated, but the sub. would not budge; then suddenly, without warning, she shot astern right out of control, careered towards the surface, and sent a splash of sea upwards only fifty yards from the *Takao*. So quickly did it happen that somehow it was not seen. A second later the bow was tilted down and hurtled back to the bottom. Fortunately this was not far, as they lay in a mere fifteen feet of clear blue water. They bumped aground, and the water began to come in.

Fraser realized that the limpet-container had not released itself as it should, which accounted for the craft being so hard to handle. He knew that no hope of escape the way they had come could be considered until it was cleared.

Magennis must already have earned his V.C., yet in spite of his exhaustion, the oxygen leak in his set, and their lying in such shallow water, he at once volunteered to leave XE3 once more and free the container—as he was an experienced diver.

Fraser said he would go, but Mick Magennis was insistent. So he set out, complete with a big spanner. Seven minutes elapsed. It was hard work to get the container free from the attachment bolts, but he managed it safely. The container rolled a bit away from the craft. Magennis groped back to the 'wet and dry' hatch and so safely aboard and into the control room for the second time. Now they could get away from this hot spot, still only yards distant from the charges laid.

Once more under control, XE3 sailed but a yard or two below the surface further, further from the scene: through the minefields, the listening hydrophone positions, the loop-detector circuit, the net-boom, and everything.

Fraser glanced at his watch. It was 2130, still the same day, and he was tiring, but they had got clear, out of range, and far beyond earshot. Had they not been, two minutes later they would have heard an explosion rend the dusk of the Singapore Straits.

The charges went off, ripping a 60-foot-long by 30-foot-wide hole in the hull of the *Takao*, putting her turrets out of action, damaging her range-finders, flooding several compartments, and altogether immobilizing her. Meanwhile, now that the worst was over, the whole quartet aboard XE3 were genuinely glad that Fraser had not wavered but persevered to lay the charges.

On and on they ploughed, at periscope depth now and again to check the course. Finally they sighted *Stygian*. By this time they had been on duty without sleep for fifty-two hours: two days and four hours. Reed was at the helm for thirty hours without a break, and they had been submerged during the day of the attack for sixteen and a half hours non-stop.

One day some time later, the wireless telegraphist aboard the base ship *Bonaventure* received the radio message that Fraser and Magennis had won the Victoria Cross. The signal came through in the early hours of the morning, about 0100; but as soon as the captain heard about it, a party swung into action and went on right through the warm spring night off the Australian shore. It was a wonderful end to a gallant adventure.

19

~~~~~~

ROBERT HAMPTON GRAY

~~~~~~

LIEUTENANT ROBERT HAMPTON GRAY, Royal Canadian
Naval Volunteer Reserve, fought right through the war—
until August 9, 1945, when Japan had actually already
lost. Fraser and Magennis earned their V.C.s on the last
day of July. The first atomic bomb fell on Hiroshima
within days of their exploit. The second within a week on
Nagasaki. It was only a matter of time before the end
came, but Gray was not to see V.J. day. By a coincidence,
he was born when the armistice was imminent in 1918.

A Canadian, Gray was the son of a jeweller in Nelson,
British Columbia. Before the war he studied for an Arts
degree at the University of British Columbia, where he
served in the Officers' Training Corps. He showed literary
leanings and became editor of the University year book.
But he never took his degree: war broke out. Gray joined
the Navy as a rating and came to England for his early
training at H.M.S. *Raleigh*. Then he made a momentous
decision. In 1940, when invasion was expected, he joined
the naval air arm. After training at H.M.S. *St Vincent* in
Gosport—across the harbour from the premier port of
Portsmouth—Gray won his wings and was promoted sub-
lieutenant in December 1940. He had a six-month spell
back in Kingston, Ontario, for further flying.

Summer 1941 brought him his first operational squadron, No. 757, which he joined at H.M.S. *Kestrel*, Winchester. Soon he was transferred to the East Indies command, and served most of the time from Kenya with three squadrons, Nos. 795, 803, and 877. Some of the time he spent on operations aboard H.M.S. *Illustrious*.

He became a lieutenant in December 1942, and then had a short spell of leave in Canada—the last time he saw his own country—followed by a refresher course. Then he was commissioned to H.M.S. *Formidable*. It was while operating from this aircraft carrier that he was mentioned in dispatches for "undaunted courage, skill, and determination in carrying out daring attacks on the German battleship *Tirpitz*." The story which had been started by Cameron and Place in their midget subs. far up the Norwegian fiord ended by the eventual destruction of her through combined attacks. So the careers of yet more of the V.C.s were interwoven in the overall pattern of the war over, on, and under the sea.

In August 1944, exactly a year before the final phase, Gray won the Distinguished Service Cross for courage and devotion to duty in air attacks on Japan.

After the atomic bombs, yet before the end of the war, he launched his last attack. There is always something especially sad about the losses in the final few days or hours of hostilities; and in Gray's case, after so courageous a career, more than ever was this true. Nothing but admiration remains for the lack of regard he showed for his own safety, especially since it was the eleventh hour of the War.

A naval airman of 'ground' staff on the flight deck of *Formidable* pulled the chocks clear of Gray's plane, which was leading Squadron 1841. He raised a hand in acknowledgment, and in seconds was gaining height over the smooth sea off Honshu, the mainland island of Japan. It was a perfectly peaceful summer's day. For a few minutes they flew in towards the coast.

"Coast ahead, sir."

Gray glanced out and down, then saw through the heat mists drifting across the coast the Bay of Onagawa Wan. He saw some five or six ships spreadeagled about the bay, and he swung the plane downward, closer and closer, till a sudden burst of anti-aircraft fire heralded a barrage from batteries based ashore, as well as concentrated shooting from five of the enemy vessels. One shot missed narrowly, and the plane shivered, shook, jumped, and flew on.

"Taking the destroyer, first," Gray told the crew.

The sound cycles of the plane increased as she tore sharply downward. The fire cracked and streamed up at them now. Everything was being telescoped into a few frantic seconds as he dived steeply to attack. There was another burst of fire and a shell struck the plane, ripping the fuselage.

"Going in low."

The firing increased and grew more accurate. Gray jerked the plane level again, a hundred feet from the destroyer straight ahead. Yet another hit was scored as Gray straightened up.

"Fire. Port wing."

"Fifty feet."

"Bombs gone."

The plane had scored a direct hit, before sailing clear of the ship and diving—for the last time—into the Bay of Onagawa Wan. As she did so the destroyer exploded amidships and sank.